HOLIDAY WALKS
in
BRITTANY

Judy Smith

Published by Sigma Leisure – an imprint of Sigma Press, 1 South Oak Lane, Wilmslow, Cheshire SK9 6AR, England.

British Library Cataloguing in Publication Data
A CIP record for this book is available from the British Library.

ISBN: 1-85058-733-7

Typesetting and Design by: Sigma Press, Wilmslow, Cheshire.

Cover design by: The Agency, Macclesfield, Cheshire

Printed by: MFP Design & Print

Cover Photographs: main cover picture - Château de la Hunaudaye; smaller pictures, from left - The alignments of Lagatjar, The harbour at Erquy, Pors Kamor on the Pink Granite Coast

Photographs: the author

Maps: Michael Gilbert

DISCLAIMER

Introducing the footpaths of Brittany

Brittany brings to mind many images – cliffs and seascapes, fishing villages and forests, folk-lore and festivals, religion, legend and pre-history. It is a land almost separate from the rest of France, temperamentally as well as geographically; a land jutting far into the Atlantic Ocean, with many miles of coastline. The unspoilt and beautiful beaches are well-known to British holiday-makers. Very much less well-known is that Brittany has more waymarked paths than any other region of France and that every Tourist Office is stocked with a good supply of maps and routes. Add to this the mild climate of Brittany – in winter, temperatures are close to those on the Côte d'Azur – and you can see that it is the ideal destination for a vacation on foot! But whether you are considering a full walking holiday in Brittany, or just want to escape from the beach for a few hours, this book should have something to offer you.

Bretons are no strangers to long-distance walking. Until a few hundred years ago, every Breton, at least once in his lifetime, was expected to undertake a walk of over 400 miles, to be completed in under a month! The walk was the famous Tro Breiz, a pilgrimage visiting each of the seven cathedrals of Brittany – Quimper, St Pol-de-Léon, Tréguier, Saint-Brieuc, Saint-Malo, Dol-de-Bretagne and Vannes. If the walk was not taken in life, the threat was that the Breton soul must take it after death, advancing along the route by one coffin length every seven years! No such heroics are demanded by the walks in this book: they are all simple circular routes between 3 and 10 miles, and many have short cuts as well, which means that most are suitable for all the family. But before you set out, here are just a few words about what you will find on foot in Brittany.

The ancient Celts perceived Brittany to be in two parts – Armor, the coast, and Argoat, the forested inland country. This simple division is apparent today. The coast is the destination of most holidaymakers and it is simply splendid! One of the most scenic footpaths in Europe, the GR 34, runs along almost the whole length of this shoreline . You could get off the boat at St Malo and follow it west to Roscoff, pick it up again on the west coast, and follow it south around Cornouaille almost to the Gulf of Morbihan – a distance of over 600 miles. If that seems a little far for a holiday, the circular walks in this book include some of the best stretches – the famous Sentier des Douaniers on the Pink Granite Coast, the beautiful Cap d'Erquy, the cliffs of the Crozon peninsula, the rocky Pointe du Grouin in the north and the wild Pointe du Raz in the west, the estuaries of the Rance and of the Trieux and lots more.

The Argoat, inland Brittany, may be something of a surprise if you have not explored it before. Brittany's spine is two ranges of hills, the Monts d'Arrée and the Montagnes Noires, hills that are older than almost any in the world. Worn down over 600 million years, the summits are now rounded humps of granite schist, broken in places by jagged outcrops of quartz. These hills are covered in wild moorland and dense forest, and cut through by deep gorges where rivers cascade in dramatic fashion, often disappearing beneath a 'chaos' of rounded boulders long since split from the granite. Walking here is on the wild side! Climb along the ridge top above the Gorges du Daoulas, trek across the moors to the lonely chapel on the high summit of Ménez-Mikel, or follow the little stream that bounces its way through the Gorges du Corong and then vanishes under the rock. A walk not to be missed is that at Huelgoat, where cascades, chasms, pools and strange rock formations are found deep in the ancient forest. Seeking more gentle scenery, you could try a ramble through the beech woods of Fougères or le Faouët, follow the valley of the Sedon with its water-mills, or stroll beside the locks of the Ille-et-Rance Canal.

But Brittany offers more than fine landscapes. This is a land where prehistoric man once walked, and he left more evidence of his occupation here than almost anywhere else in Europe. Many of the routes in this book pass by a megalith or an ancient burial chamber of some kind, often in a remote place, accessible only on foot. Walking in the region of the Abers, you will find some of the tallest standing stones in all France. Far away in the east of Brittany, a walk across the moors brings you to the most amazing collection of megaliths at St Just.

Above everything else, Brittany is a Celtic land – a land that has much in common with Cornwall and Wales and Ireland, a land reviving its ancient language (a few relevant words are included in this book), an enchanted land full of mythology and legend and superstition. Almost every walk has a story attached to some part of it. The Devil makes his presence known all over the place – every cave is a 'Grotte du Diable' and at one of these (in le Châtellier) you can even see smoke rising as the Devil fries his pancakes! The legend of the ill-fated lovers Tristan and Isolde has cast its spell on the west coast, and the Bay of Douarnenez is home to the story of the lost city of Ys, Brittany's answer to Atlantis. The Breton troubadours of the Middle Ages set the stories of King Arthur and the Knights of the Round Table in the forest of Paimpont – it became the Brocéliande of the legend. You can walk in the woods to find the Château de Comper, the home of the Lady of the Lake, seek out Merlin's seat on the edge of the Valley of no Return, visit the Fountain of Barenton where Merlin first met the Fairy Viviane – and sample the waters of the Fountain of Youth which he drank to keep at bay the signs of his advancing years!

There are so many fine walks in Brittany that choosing among them has proved extremely difficult. If you think of each route in this book as a taste of walking in that area, you can also explore the 'More Walks' section to find your own favourites. The friendly Tourist Information Offices of Brittany should be able to provide you with all the walking routes mentioned – and if you are worried about the French text, the 'Dictionary of Walking Words' might shed some light. Tourist Offices can also be very helpful if you explain that you need a bus or a taxi to drop you at some point 10 miles down the line to enjoy a quiet walk home along a Grande Randonnée – France is far more orientated towards the rambler than most of us imagine. In addition, the Tourist Offices supply a wealth of information on places of interest in an area. With each walk I have included just a few suggestions – often of places associated with the walk, or with special appeal to walkers.

I have enjoyed exploring again the paths of Brittany for this book. Special thanks are due to Eric, my husband, who walked every one of the routes with me (sometimes more than once) and was (reasonably!) patient with my desire to visit every walk mentioned in the 'More Walks' sections as well: in one year we must have covered more than 800 miles on foot! I am also grateful to the friends and acquaintances who have helped with all manner of enquiries. My thanks go also to the Offices du Tourisme of Brittany – they were more than generous with time and information and I am sure that they will help you in the same way.

I hope you will enjoy this very different journey through Brittany. It only remains to wish you *Chañs vat deoc'h!* – and you can work that one out for yourselves!

Judy Smith

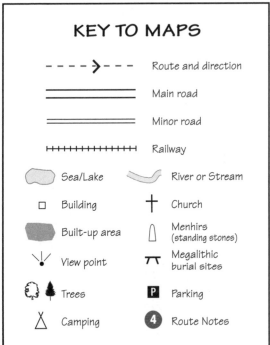

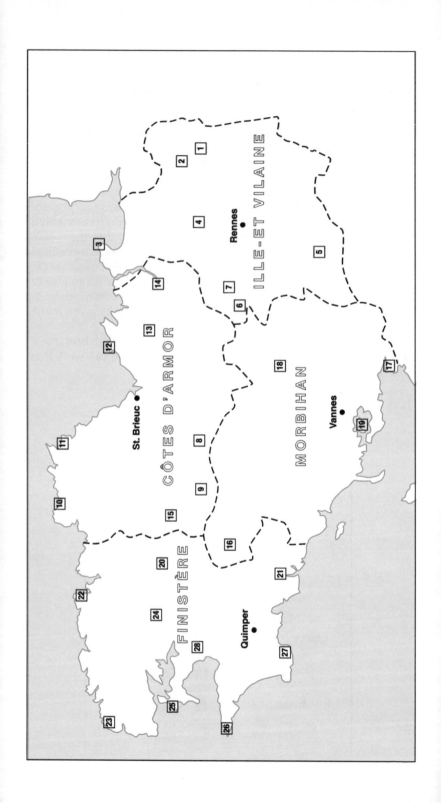

Contents

Walking in France

France is almost certainly the best country for walking in Europe: the scenery is widely varied, the tracks are well-maintained and well-waymarked and every Office du Tourisme can offer you an assortment of routes and inexpensive maps of the area.

The excellence of the footpaths of France is due almost entirely to an organisation called the Fédération Française de la Randonnée Pédestre – The FFRP – who over the last half century have waymarked and described routes of all kinds throughout France. Many of the walks in this book are based on their routes, and you will undoubtedly be grateful for some of their waymarking as you follow them. Their long distance paths, the Grandes Randonnées (GR), are the best waymarked paths imaginable, and will invariably lead you past all the most interesting features and best viewpoints in an area. If there is something worth seeing, the Grande Randonnée will take you there. Next there are the Grandes Randonnées du Pays (GRP), round tours of an area or region which may take, in walking time, anything from a couple of days to a week. They aim to show you the best a region has to offer. Finally, there are the Petites Randonnées (PR), the equivalent of our short circular walks, and these are sprinkled generously over the whole country. Each of these route types has its own waymarks, painted on trees, rocks, telegraph poles, or any other convenient surface – the Grandes Randonnées are marked white on red, the Grandes Randonnées du Pays yellow on red and the Petites Randonnées, yellow. You will meet all of them on the walks in this book, so here is all you need to know:

Path continues   *Wrong way*   *Left turn*   *Right turn*

Thus you are warned of every turn before you reach it, and halted by a cross if you have missed it. Nothing could be simpler! In fairness, it must be said that although Grandes Randonnées are invariably superbly waymarked, the state of a Petite Randonnée may reflect the level of enthusiasm of the local tourist board or walking group. Even so, most are excellent. To accompany these fine routes, the FFRP produces a series of Topoguides, which offer all the relevant information from flora and fauna to history, geology and details of available refreshment. The pity is that only very few have been translated into English, and, oddly, these are generally of the long distance routes. For the rest, at least a working knowledge of French is needed. If you decide to tackle these – or any other described routes – a vocabulary of 'walking words in French' has been included in this book to help you.

Another excellent feature of walking in France is that most paths are open to you – only those marked 'Privé' deny you access. It is accepted that you will not wander on crops or gardens and that you will not leave litter or pick flowers. It should be mentioned that, in winter, some forest paths are temporarily closed for the period of 'la chasse' – the hunting season – generally from November to February, but these paths will again be marked. In France, farmers and landowners seem much more in tune with walkers than in England and will generally greet you cheerfully. If you can manage just a 'Bonjour' in return, it is certain to go down well.

And now, the footpaths of France await you – and they are guaranteed to be addictive! Take one short stretch of a Grande Randonnée and you may well be hooked for life. It remains only to wish you 'Bonne route!'

A little history to set the scene

The Megalithic Period

The multitude of megaliths are obvious signs of Brittany's early occupation, but little is known of the people who built them. Most are dated between 5000 and 2000 BC and of these the dolmens and gallery graves are generally the earliest while the menhirs, standing alone or in alignments, tend to date from around the end of this period. The east-west orientation of many alignments and the discovery of primitive 'calendars' (see the Tribunal on the walk at St. Just) suggest that these people were sun-worshippers and early farmers who needed to predict the seasons. They were also people who were fascinated with the after-life. The latest megaliths (from the Bronze Age, 1800 – 600 BC) have yielded jewellery, decorated pottery and other artefacts now to be found in the museums at Vannes and Rennes.

Celts and Romans

Around 600 BC the first wave of Celts arrived in Brittany – they called the country Armor, the Land of the Sea. Warlike and tribal, they were also farmers. They were subjugated by the Romans after their most prominent tribe the Veneti lost the epic sea battle of 56 BC . The Romans brought civilisation, but little remains to be seen of their occupation (although you can see the vestiges of a Roman aqueduct on a walk near Maël-Carhaix). Armor became the Roman Armorica.

In the fifth century AD, the Roman legions were recalled to fight battles nearer home, leaving France – and Britain – vulnerable to invaders. Tribes of Angles and Saxons pushed Britain's population to the south-west – and from there, across the sea to Armorica. From Ireland, Wales and Cornwall came the second wave of Celts, and they called their new country Brittany – little Britain. These Celts were a Christian people. They soon converted their adopted land - and provided the country with its abundance of saints.

The Duchy of Brittany

In 799, Brittany was seized by Charlemagne, who gave his friend Nominoë the title 'Duke of Brittany'. Nominoë's son, Erispoë, went one step farther and called himself King. Brittany was a kingdom for a mere hundred years. After the death of King Alain Barbe-Torte in 952, there followed around 400 years of trouble and disorder, culminating in the War of the Succession. In 1364, the Montforts (supported by England) emerged victorious, restored order to Brittany and ensured its prosperity for the next hundred years. The famous Breton warrior du Guesclin fought on the French side in this war and eventually became Constable of France.

Throughout this time, Brittany was a Duchy independent of France. In 1483, the redoubtable Anne of Brittany succeeded to the Duchy and eight years later, married Charles VIII, King of France. When he died in an accident, she went on to marry his brother, Louis XII – but still she retained independence for Brittany. After her death, the Duchy passed to her daughter Claude – who, after her marriage to the future François I of France, relinquished her birthright. In 1532, the union of Brittany and France was ratified at the Parliament of Vannes.

French Brittany

Brittany was given a French governor and a parliamentary assembly in Nantes. Initially the new province prospered. In 1534 the Breton explorer Jacques Cartier discovered Canada. This was an affluent period when many elaborate chateaux sprang up and religious building and art flourished (see the Parish Closes in the Monts d'Arrée - near the walk up Ménez Mikel). In 1610 Louis XIII acceded to the throne and began the stripping of the vast forests of the interior to build warships. But it was after the accession of Louis XIV in 1643 that things really began to go wrong. Heavy taxes were demanded to fund the King's extravagant tastes and the people began to rebel. The famous 'Stamped Paper Revolt' of 1675 (a rebellion against tax on all paper used for legal documents) was squashed with much bloodshed. Pewter and tobacco were taxed and an army of peasants calling themselves the Bonnets Rouges (Redcaps) rampaged through Brittany. The rebellion was crushed with excessive brutality. From this period came Vauban, soldier and military architect and, at least initially, a friend of Louis XIV. His fortifications are seen all around the coasts of Brittany (and indeed elsewhere in France). On these walks you will meet him at Carantec and Camaret, Perros-Guirec and Cap Fréhel, among others. He too became disillusioned with the Royalists and fell from favour before he died in 1707.

The French Revolution

Brittany continued to resent its French domination, and in the 18th century, was pleased initially to support the Revolutionaries against the king and aristocracy. But soon it became apparent that the new regime brought yet more problems for Brittany. Now the Revolutionaries made laws against the Priests, threatened the Breton language and demanded conscription to the army of a country to which the Bretons felt no allegiance. The despotic governor Carrier drowned thousands of supposed Royalists in the Loire. So arose the *Association Bretonne* – the anti-Revolutionary movement popularly known as the Chouans. Their name derived from *chat huant*, the cry of the screech owl, which they used as a night-time signal. The last Chouan was executed in 1804 but the Bretons still tell stories of their exploits and there are many markers and memorials. After the *Reign of Terror*, Napoleon and his victories brought some peace and pride to France – and to Brittany too – and the final Breton revolt was squashed in 1832.

More recent history

The 19th century saw the decline of Brittany's fishing industry and the conversion of much of the wild moorland to agriculture. Brittany began to re-assert its unique identity and folklore and festivals were again promoted. Two great Breton writers of this time were Chateaubriand and Jules Verne. Artists flocked to experience the wildness of Brittany, among them Gauguin and his school of synthetists who lodged at Pont-Aven in the 1880s.

The early 20th century brought the Great War in which Brittany suffered greatly. Being a seafaring people, its men joined the Navy – and Brittany lost a larger part of its population than any other region of France. In World War II its role was glorious – Bretons eagerly responded to de Gaulle's cry to join the Free French army, and indeed a quarter of that force were Breton. The Breton Resistance was active and operated many escape routes across the Channel. The main ports of Brittany, Brest, St. Nazaire, Lorient and St. Malo were all destroyed.

Soon after the war's end, a new committee was formed to safeguard the interests of Brittany – the *Comité d'Études et de Liaisons des Intérêts Bretons*. This was a turning point for the economy of Brittany and for her nationalism. The Breton flag had been designed by Morvan Marchal back in 1926. Called the Gwenn ha du (white and black)), it is the only flag not to use colour. It can be seen flying all over Brittany from public buildings to boats in the harbours. In schools the language is again promoted and it is estimated more than 300.000 people speak Breton. Traditional folk music is heard in the many festivals. Since 1985, bi-lingual road signs have been introduced.

Tourism

Brittany's tourist industry has grown since the last war and no doubt benefitted from the splendid images portrayed in *Monsieur Hulot's Holiday!* The coastline is still almost entirely unspoiled, and completely lacking in the more garish trappings of commercialism that have invaded many British resorts. The beaches of Brittany are perfect for a family holiday, and both coast and inland are gaining a reputation for walking with a wealth of published itineraries. Nearly a million Britons now visit Brittany every year, making it one of our most popular holiday destinations.

A few words in Breton:

Aber	estuary
Amann	butter
Aven	river
Beg	point or summit
Bihan	small
Bras	big
Breizh	Brittany
C'hi	dog
Du	black
Enez	island
Fest-noz	night festival
Groaz	cross
Gwenn	white
Gwin	wine
Kastel	castle
Ker	town, village, hamlet
Lan	monastery, hermitage
Lann	heath
Loc	remote place, hermitage
Loc'h	lagoon, coastal lake
Men	stone, rock
Menez	mountain
Meur	large, important
Mor	sea
Nevez	new
Palud	marsh
Penn	head, end, summit
Plou	parish
Pors	port
Roc'h	rock, crag
Ruz	red
Ti / ty	house
Unan, daou, tri, pevar, pemp	one, two, three, four, five

And phrases to use yourselves:

Cheers / Good Health!	Yec'hed mat!
Thank you!	Trugarez!
Goodbye!	Kenavo!
Good morning/afternoon	Demat
Good night	Noz vat

Dictionary of French Walking Words

anse	a cove, a small bay
atteindre	to reach
balisage	waymarking
bifurquer	to fork
blanc	white
bleu(e)	blue
bois	a wood
bosquet	a spinney, a copse
chemin	a way, a path
colline	a hill
contourner	to go around, to skirt
creux	sunken or hollowed out
dessous	under
dessus	above
droit (tout droit)	straight ahead
droite	right
église	church
empierré	stony or metalled (as in road)
emprunter	to take (as in direction)
étang	a pond, a pool
en face	opposite
fourche	a fork
franchir	to clear, to cross
gauche	left
goudronnée	tarmacked
grimper	to climb
hameau	hamlet
jaune	yellow
jusqu'à	as far as
longer	to skirt
mener	to lead
monter	to climb
niveau	a level
patte d'oie	multiple path or road junction
pente	slope
prairie	a meadow
rouge	red
route	a road, track or direction
ruisseau	a stream
sentier	a footpath, a track
sous-bois	undergrowth
suivre	to follow
talus	a slope or bank
tourner	to turn
traverser	to cross
variante	alternative route
vert(e)	green
virer	to bend or turn

Offices du Tourisme

Walk	Location	Address	How to find it
1/2	Fougères	1, place Aristide Briand, 35300 FOUGÈRES	Beside the Jardin Public and the Église St Léonard.
3	Cancale	44, rue du Port, BP 50, 35260 CANCALE	Just off the main square, on the road to the port.
4	Hédé	Maison du Canal d'Ille-et-Rance, La Madeleine, Bazouges-sous- Hédé, 35630 HÉDÉ	Beside the canal at la Madeleine. There is also an Office du Tourisme in the town of Tinténiac.
5	Redon	Place de la République, 35600 REDON	In the pedestrianised centre, beside the railway overpass.
6/7	Plélan-le-Grand (Brocéliande)	37, avenue de la Libération, 35380 PLÉLAN-le-GRAND	On the main road through Plélan at its eastern end.
8/9	Mûr-de-Bretagne	Place de l'Église – BP 16, 22530 MÛR-de-BRETAGNE	A modern building in the central square opposite the church.
10	Perros-Guirec	21, Place de l'Hôtel de Ville – BP 54, 22700 PERROS-GUIREC	On the main road in the centre of the town.
11	Paimpol	Mairie de Paimpol, Rue Pierre Feutren, 22500 PAIMPOL	In the town centre.
12	Erquy	Bd. de la Mer 'Le Rial', 22430 ERQUY	On the sea front at Erquy.
13	Jugon-les-Lacs	Place du Martray, 22270 JUGON-les-LACS	In the town square.
14	Dinan	6, rue de l'Horloge, BP 261, 22105 DINAN	In the centre of town, very close to the bell tower.
15	Vannes	1, rue Thiers, 56000 VANNES	From the centre of the town, head downhill towards the port.
16	le Faouët	1, Rue de Quimper, 56320 le FAOUËT	Just off the central square (Place des Halles), on the road to Scaër.
17	Pénestin	Allée du Grand Pré, BP 7, 56760 PÉNESTIN	On the road out of town towards Assérac.
18	Guéhenno	Place de la Congrégation, 56120 JOSSELIN	In the town, just above the castle.
19	Pont-Aven	5, Place de l'Hôtel de Ville, BP 36, 29930 PONT-AVEN	In the main square of the town.
20	Huelgoat	Place Alphonse Penven, BP 19, 29690 HUELGOAT	In the Moulin du Chaos, at the end of the lake.
21	Locarn	Locarn Tourisme et Culture, 19, Place du Centre, 22340 LOCARN	Just off the village square.
22	Carantec	4, Rue Pasteur BP 62, 29660 CARANTEC	Near the church.
23	The Abers	14, Place le Flô, 29260 LESNEVEN	In the centre of the town.
24	Sizun	3, Rue de l'Argoat, 29450 SIZUN	Off the square, just opposite the church.

25	Camaret-sur-Mer	15, Quai Kléber – BP 16, 29570 CAMARET-SUR-MER	On the sea-front, facing the harbour.
26	Audierne	8, Rue Victor Hugo, 29770 AUDIERNE	In the square beside the harbour. There is also an Office du Tourisme in the complex at the Pointe du Raz.
27	Loctudy	Place des Anciens Combattans – BP 22, 29750 LOCTUDY	In the square of the car park.
28	Châteaulin	Quay Cosmao, 29150 CHÂTEAULIN	On the quayside.

Recommended Publications

Michelin Tourist Guide to Brittany. ISBN 2-06-131404-X

Landscapes of Brittany, Rodney Ansell (Sunflower Books) ISBN 1-85691-025-3

Essential Explorer - Brittany (AA) ISBN 0-7495-1024-2

And in French only – *Découvrir la Bretagne en marchant*, Dominique Le Brun (Éditions Franck Mercier) ISBN 2-86868-137-9

Brittany on the Internet

There are literally hundreds of web sites about Brittany. Here are just a few you might find useful.

www.ffrp.asso.fr: This is the website of the French rambling association, the Fédération Française de la Randonnée Pédestre (FFRP). Along with other information (in French), the site lists and describes the major Topoguides and gives information on ordering direct – a cheaper option than buying in England.

www.brittany-ferries.com: The website of Brittany Ferries, giving sailing schedules, prices, online reservations and details of holiday properties all over Brittany (and elsewhere)

www.brittanytourism.com: The official tourist site offering history, language (a list of common words), property rentals, brochures, links to departmental tourist offices and just about anything else.

www.brittany-guide.com: Another interesting site giving travel information, weather-forecasts, a neatly-potted history and accommodation details

www.smo.uhi.ac.uk/saoghal/mion-chanain/brezhoneg: This is the site of Sabhal Mòr Ostaig, the college for the development of the Gaelic language – the above will take you directly to their Breton site. Here you can take online lessons in Breton and refer to an English-Breton dictionary.

Opposite: lighthouse off Point du Grouin

Ille-et-Vilaine

1. In the Forest of Fougères

Fougères is known for its fine medieval castle – and for its splendid beech forest where history, legend and recreation all have their part. This short walk visits a prehistoric dolmen, a Roman hill fort and the site of an ancient healing tree – and returns to a lake where you can picnic and swim.

Grade: Easy

Distance: 5km (3 miles)

Time: 1¼ hours

Map: IGN Série Bleue 1317 E – but the map of the forest provided by Tourist Information is quite adequate.

Start and finish: Ferme de Chênedet in the forest of Fougères

How to get there: From Fougères, take the D177 north-east in the direction of St-Hilaire-du-Harcouët. Once in the forest, turn left at the cross-roads, S.P. Chênedet (approx. 3km from Fougères). On reaching the farm and equestrian centre, the road bears right, and there are then several small parking areas on the left, before the T-junction. From these, the lake can be seen a short distance away, through the trees.

Refreshment: There are no refreshment facilities in the forest. Of course, there are many eating places in Fougères.

Notes: This is an easy, short walk that can be undertaken by anyone. Nevertheless, you should note that the forest can be muddy in winter – or after very wet weather. Choose your footwear accordingly. The lake makes a pleasant place to start and end your walk, and in summer swimming is possible from the sandy beach. Don't forget your costume – and the sun cream. For the young (at least in heart) an excellent *parcours sportif* (fitness course) encircles the lake.

Waymarking: Grande Randonnée waymarkings (white on red) at first, followed by yellow dots (briefly) and then orange.

Introduction

'I would like to ask everyone, have you seen Fougères?' So wrote Victor Hugo two centuries ago after he visited the town that was to be the setting for one of his novels. It is easy to understand his enthusiasm – there cannot be a more magnificent castle anywhere than that at Fougères. Its dark walls, turrets, watch towers, moat and drawbridge are the epitome of medieval military architecture. Seen floodlit on a winter's night, its thirteen conical towers rising eerily from the river mists, it is guaranteed to send a shiver down even the most well-insulated spine!

Fougères itself was a sort of frontier town, on the border between Brittany and the rest of France. It was the town that saw the start of the Chouan movement, the resistance of the Royalists of Brittany to the

Cordon of Druids, Forest of Fougères

French Revolutionaries. In truth, the Bretons were not so much Royalists as a people resisting conscription to an army of a country to which they felt no allegiance. Balzac chose Fougères as the setting for his historical tale `Les Chouans', and Victor Hugo's 'Quatre-Vingt-Treize' likewise told of the uprising of 1793. Fougères is a town steeped in history.

To the north of the town lies a vast forest of beech and oak, and this also has its connections with the Chouans. At one forest entrance, a cross stands marking their first encounter with the Revolutionary forces. In the woods nearby you can see the steps and gateway to the cellars of Landéan, dating from the 12th century. They were built by Raoul II, Baron of Fougères, to conceal his possessions from the English under Henry II. More treasure was said to be hidden deep in the forest under the *Pierre du Trésor*. This huge stone unfortunately collapsed when someone clumsily decided to seek his fortune! The well laid out forest trails visit these and other historical and legendary sites – a Roman camp, dolmens, a line of standing stones, the vestiges of a convent and some ancient fortifications are scattered in the undergrowth, while through the heart of the forest runs the old salt-smugglers road. In medieval times, salt was not taxed in Brittany, making its cost a mere twentieth of that over the border. This route through the forest was preferable to the main road for the smugglers, but even so, it was the scene of many bloodthirsty encounters with customs officers.

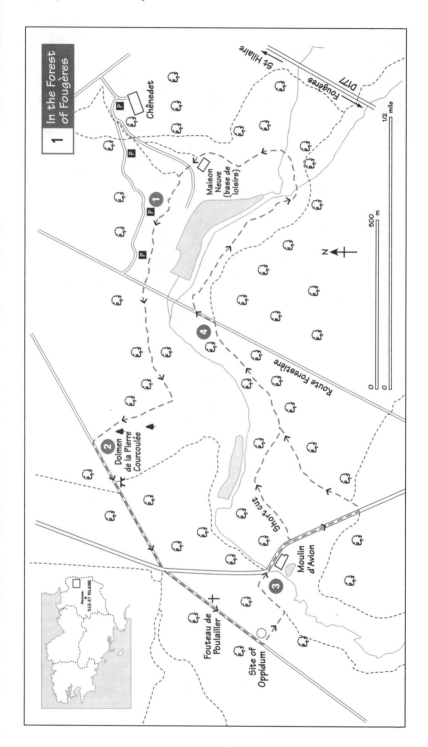

In the Forest of Fougères

1

Chênedet

Maison Neuve (base de loisirs)

St Hilaire

Fougères

D177

1/2 mile

500 m

N

Route Forestière

Dolmen de la Pierre Courcoulée

Short cut

Moulin d'Avion

Fouteau de Poulailler

Site of Oppidum

Rennes

ILLE-ET-VILAINE

The route chosen for this walk is a compound of several marked trails. Deep in the forest is a lake where bathing and canoeing are possible in summer – a bonus if you have children with you. Starting from this lake, you follow a Grande Randonnée through beech and pine woods to reach a prehistoric site known as the *Dolmen de la Pierre Courcoulée* or the 'Huguenot Stone'. This huge dolmen, now broken in two and sunken into the ground, once stood high on twelve legs. Breton forests are always places of legend, and soon you pass a cross that marks the site of a long-gone much-venerated beech tree, the *Fouteau de Poulailler*. To ensure recovery from illness, peasants would dance around the tree sweeping the ground with a holly branch, and place an egg between its roots. Pieces of bark taken from the tree helped with the cure. A little farther up the hill, the remains of an oppidum, a Roman hill fort, can be found in the undergrowth. After passing a restored old mill, the way returns through the woodland, and you can look out for deer and wild boar – and the mischievous forest goblin. If you should see him, the advice is to leave him well alone!

The Walk

1. From any of the parking spaces, walk through the trees towards the lake. In doing so, you will cross a broad path, which is the route of the Grande Randonnée – white on red flashes can be seen on the trees. Turn right on this path and follow it as it weaves through the woods. The path crosses directly over a stony track and soon crosses a stream on a log bridge. Shortly afterwards, on reaching a plantation of conifers, the route turns sharp right – look out for the waymarks! Five minutes walking through the conifers brings you to a wide stony track. Here you turn left, and shortly, on the left, find the *Dolmen de la Pierre Courcoulée*.

2. Now continue along the stony track to the cross-roads at its end – the Carrefour de Poulailler. Here cross the road and, now leaving the GR, bear left uphill, on the Route Forestière des Courbes. After about 200 metres, you reach the cross marking the site of the *Fouteau de Poulailler*. Continue up the hill, and as you reach the summit, look out for a long ridge mound in the undergrowth on the left. This is the wall of the oppidum, and you should turn left on a rather overgrown track going right through it. The track heads steeply downhill and soon meets a wide earthen track that is part of the V.T.T. route – yellow flashes. Turn left on this track, which after about 150 metres, bears right to come down to a road.

3. Turn right on this road, cross over the stream and pass the mill (Moulin d'Avion). The path you are now seeking is the orange-marked bridleway, which turns left from this road in about 250 metres. If the road seems too busy – or you fancy a forest

adventure – take instead the first path on the left after the mill, just as the road corners right. This brings you into a rough field full of beech trees. In this field, keep straight ahead, parallel to the wall on your left – you will see a yellow dot on a tree. When the wall ends, the track bears to the right – at this point there are, of course, no dots in sight! Nevertheless, continue on this rather vague track, and just as you begin to think you have got it all wrong, suddenly yellow dots appear all around you. They now lead you on to meet the bridleway, which is a rather narrow, earthy, obvious track. Turn left on it and now you have orange dots to follow through the forest. This is not always easy, as ivy and other foliage obscure many of them. But eventually you emerge on a stony road.

4. Here turn left, and after about 60 metres on this road, turn right on a track that heads for the lake. After crossing a little stream, you meet the path that encircles the lake. The *parcours sportif* runs alongside, so if you are feeling that this short walk has not really given you enough exercise, you are now in a position to do something about it. Continue following this path to the right. At the far end of the lake, it swings away through an attractive spinney before returning to the lakeside buildings. Here leave the track (the track ahead here was part of the old salt-smugglers road) and keep beside the earthen wall behind the wooden buildings. After crossing the tarmac road, you again pick up the markings of the GR, and from there can return to your car.

More Walks in the Area

There are 4 colour-coded waymarked trails in the forest, each about 5km in length. These walks are all very suitable for families as the terrain is easy and children love hunting for the spots of colour on the trees. The walks start from different points and each is based on features of interest. The Office du Tourisme in Fougères produce a first-class forest map showing all the trails and describing the wildlife and many historical sites.

The area around Fougères itself is superb for walking. The Office du Tourisme has an excellent booklet *Au Pays de Fougères*, which describes briefly all the interesting places and walks in the area – and there are many. This booklet does not give directions – for these, you can pick up some of the many free or inexpensive leaflets that have been prepared. Most of the routes have no text and are intended to be followed using map and waymarkings only. This may make you feel a little uneasy, but treated as something of an adventure, it is usually successful!

The area around Antrain and the valley of the River Couesnon (here the boundary with Normandy) is most pleasant and here there are several well-marked circuits through the woods and beside the river. Ask for the collection of leaflets entitled *Les Sentiers du Pays Gallo*.

One route that is, of course, very well-waymarked is the GR 34 that passes right through the forest. Following this in a north-westerly direction, the route is very attractive, and in 12km you come to the old granite town of St Germain-en-Coglès, which is itself surrounded by woodland. From here, you could get a taxi to take you back to Fougères – enquire at the Office du Tourisme before you go. Another 16km along the way (quite a long walk now!) you come to the town of St-Brice-en-Coglès from which a bus service runs to Fougères. Another possibility is to follow the GR south-east to Dompierre-du-Chemin (24km), also an interesting town. As no leaflets are produced for these GR routes, you would need to buy the regional IGN map, or, for more details, a Topoguide – *Côte d'Émeraude (Ref. 345)* is the one for this area. Although Topoguides are relatively expensive, they are much cheaper to obtain in France than England – and if you become an enthusiast, this one will guide you all the way up to the coast and along to St Brieuc.

And finally, if you are in this area, Walk 2 starts just 10km from Fougères at the fascinating hilltop village of le Châtellier, from which there is a view over the whole of the region.

Places of interest nearby

The town of Fougères has much to offer. Behind the magnificent castle is the exquisite Gothic church of St Sulpice with its slender spire and, all around, are medieval streets whose names evoke the professions of those who lived here long ago. A sharp climb from the Rue de Lusignan will bring you to the Butte à Bigot from which there are excellent views.

From the other side of the castle, ramparts with walks and gardens lead up to the town above. Here the 18th century Rue Nationale leads to the Église de St Léonard – and the Jardin Public from which there is another fine view of the castle. The Office du Tourisme is just beside the Jardin Public and it is worth asking for their 'Town Trail' leaflet *Circuit de la Vieille Ville*. Yellow flashes will guide you on a 2km tour of the main sights.

Leaving the town and heading for the provinces, you are everywhere struck by the mix of legend and history in this region. At Dompierre to the south is a valley where a gap between huge rocks is known as the *Saut Roland*. Roland, one-time Prefect of the Marches of Brittany, tried three times to jump the gap on his horse. The third time he was unlucky, and fell to his death. An imprint of a horse-shoe marks the spot. Not far away is the *pierre degoûttante*, where water falls continuously into a hollow rocky basin – the water is said to be the tears of Roland's beloved, crying until judgement day. Nearby also, a rock closes the entrance to an underground cavern of treasures – it can be opened only by using a hazel stick on the morning of St Jean's day! And even this will not get you very far, since the entrance is then guarded by a dragon!

Near Noyal-sous-Bazouges there is a huge stone known as *le Pierre Longue*. It was apparently dropped by the devil on his way to build St Michael's Mount. In fact, it is a menhir, now topped by a cross in an attempt to 'Christianise' the pagan site. Near Louvigné-du-Désert in the north are rocks where St Guillaume stayed seven years – you can see his bed, his, fountain, his bowl, and the marks of his knees. Near St-Germain-en-Coglès is a rock that comes down to the water to drink at midnight on Christmas Eve – it conceals treasure, but misfortune comes to those who see it. The whole area is full of these legends. Equip yourselves with the leaflet *Pierres et Sites Légendaires* (unfortunately, only in French) and go out hunting.

2. History and legend at le Châtellier

This is a walk in the traditional countryside of the Normandy border – sunken lanes, woodland, farms and fields of brown and white cattle. Le Châtellier boasts, from its church spire, a view of 37 more, and in the woodland below, a rock inhabited by the devil himself!

Grade: Easy

Distance: 7.5km (4¾ miles). Short circuit of 2km also possible.

Time: 2½ hours (approx. three-quarters of an hour for short circuit)

Map: IGN Série Bleue 1317 E

Start and finish: The church at le Châtellier

How to get there: From Fougères, head north on the D758. After about 9km, turn left where sign-posted to le Châtellier. The church is at the top of the hill.

Refreshment: There is a pleasant bar/restaurant in le Châtellier. For other facilities, you would need to go into Fougères.

Notes: Out of season or in wet weather, some of the lanes on this walk will be muddy – think of good footwear. In a dry summer, there should be no problem. There is no possibility of refreshment en route, so it may be advisable to carry water on a hot day. The walk passes the *Parc Floral* – the gardens of the Château de la Folletière – and you might be interested in visiting them. They are open every day in summer.

Waymarking: The route is waymarked in white throughout.

The Walk

This is a walk to take after wet weather. And if that seems a little surprising, it does have its explanation. On the slopes of the hill below le Châtellier is a huge rock from whose cleft, at certain times, a spiral of 'smoke' is seen to rise. Do not for one moment think this is anything to do with atmospherics – it is obviously the Devil himself frying his pancakes. But perhaps he is hungrier after the weather changes. This rock and its legend are well-known, but even so there are no signs and no publicity – if you see smoke rising from the frying-pan, you are likely to be the only witness!

The devil plays his part in another story connected with le Châtellier, this time more history than legend. Le Châtellier stands on the summit of a steep wooded hill. In the middle of the 19th century, only a narrow path ran through the woodland, making it difficult for the residents of the villages at the foot of the hill to reach le Châtellier. The woodland was owned by one Dupontavice de St Germain, who refused to give up any of his land to make a wider path. In anger at being asked, he closed the existing path! The villagers could take no more, and one May night, twenty-five of their young men got together and as soon as it was dark began felling trees and creating a path. By dawn, the deed was done and a fine wide track led to the church on the hilltop. The next day being Sunday, all the villagers delighted in climbing the new route to attend Mass. Dupontavice was furious, but when questioned, each of the villagers said he had been asleep in bed and had not even heard a tree fall. It had obviously been the work of the devil! And so it was called the Chemin du Diable and in the last century it became the tarmacked road that now leads steeply up to the church.

Le Châtellier stands on the highest hill around and it is said that from the church on a clear day, you can not only see 37 spires, but also Mont St Michel, far away on the coast. So perhaps a fine day after rain is what you are looking for on this walk. From le Châtellier the route leads through countryside that is most attractive and in some ways more akin to Normandy than to Brittany. Pleasantly rolling, with interspersed pastures and woodland, it is a region of large farms and fields where brown and white 'bespectacled' cattle graze. The route encircles the Château de la Folletière, a fine château surrounded by woodland in which is concealed a grotto with a shrine. The château has fine floral gardens, which can be visited in summer. The return takes you through the woods and past the Roche au Diable – be on your guard if you see the smoke rising! But if the devil is not at home, there is just one more story you might like to test out. Below the rock is a cave, and from this, a narrow passage runs underneath. Legend has it that all the young girls who cross the passage under the Roche au Diable before Trinity will marry within the year – perhaps a better guarantee than trying to catch a bouquet!

Château de la Folletière

The Walk

1. From the church at le Châtellier, walk downhill towards the village. Just before the road junction, look for a cross on your left and take the broad track beside it. The track soon becomes grassy and heads quite steeply downhill. Continue on this track beneath the chestnut trees all the way to the bottom of the hill, where you will find a red arrow on a tree pointing to the left, and a white arrow pointing to the right. If you would like to take just the short circuit, follow the red flashes around the bottom of the hill to reach the road. Here turn left and in about 100 metres you arrive at point 6, where you look for a path on the left.

   For the main walk, turn right, and after about 15 metres, bear left keeping the stream on your left. The white flashes now guide you around to the D19, which you cross diagonally to the right. The path now descends, and in the woodland, crosses a little stream on a bridge called the Pont Chauvin.

2. Now climb on a sunken track to reach the hamlet of la Chauvinaie. Here bear right following a yellow (!) arrow. This track takes you to the farm of la Verdaie, where you pass between the farm buildings and continue to the T-junction. Here turn left (no signs visible) and continue on this tarmacked road to the cross-roads. Cross straight over in the direction of Guémenard. After about 300 metres, you reach a sort of crossroads where a cross (the Croix aux Chats – but why?) hides itself in the undergrowth on the left. Bear left, continuing on a tarmacked road.

3. Where the road bends right, a broad track continues ahead under the beech trees – again waymarked with a yellow flash. Ahead to the left, you can see the handsome Château de la Folletière and behind you, the church at le Châtellier dominates the scene. Just before the gate to the château, double back to the right following the waymarks into the wood. Soon a little path on the right leads you to the Grotte de la Folletière with its shrine. Having seen this, retrace your steps a few metres to the path you have just left. Now turn right uphill (even though there is a yellow cross on a tree), pass some rocks, and continue to meet a sunken track where you can see another farm across a field ahead. Here turn right and continue to the road. Turn left and follow the road to the farm of Guémenard.

4. Here an arrow tells you to bear left on a broad stony track. Just as this track bears right, take instead a broad grassy track on the left with trees on either side. Passing the farm on your right, keep ahead to the big wall. Here turn right and keep left around the end of the wall to meet the stony road leading to the château and its gardens – the Parc Floral. Turn right away from the château and then left on the tarmacked road.

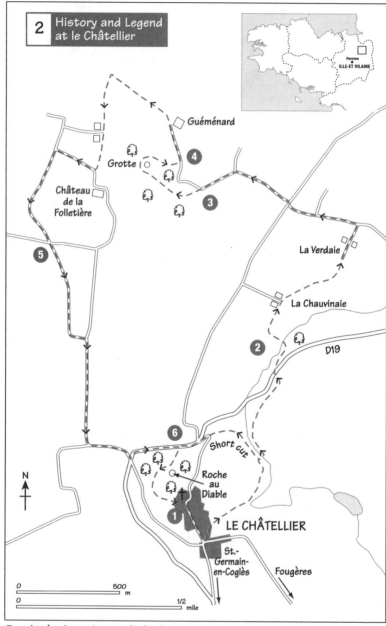

Guéménard

Grotte

4

3

Château
de la
Folletière

5

La Verdaie

La Chauvinaie

2

D19

6

Short cut

Roche
au
Diable

1

LE CHÂTELLIER

St.-
Germain-
en-Coglès

Fougères

N

0   500
0   m
0   1/2
mile

5. At the junction with the larger road, continue ahead (i.e. left) and
    keep to this road for over1km to the T-junction at the bottom of
    the hill. Here turn left, and after 200 metres or so, look for a path
    in the trees on the right

6. Follow this waymarked path (red and white now) uphill through

the woods. Take care, as you will soon pass the Roche au Diable on your left. Continuing on the path, bear left before_the red waymarks on the trees and continue to follow them uphill. Reaching the church wall at the top, bear right to return to the square.

More Walks in the Area

Le Châtellier is only about 6 miles from Fougères, where there are several walks in the fine beech forest with many historical sites – see Walk 1. The Office du Tourisme in Fougères can provide you with a good map of the forest trails.

At Le Châtellier, you are very close to St Germain-en Coglès (about 3km) with its attractive woods. Two circuits are described and waymarked from St Germain, and both are pleasant walks full of interest. The first is a short walk of 6km (and even this has a short cut) which heads for the village of Marigny where there is a pool and fine 16th century chapel. The way back takes you past a rock with an interesting legend. You are hardly likely to be contemplating this walk at midnight on Christmas Eve. But, if you were, you would see this rock descend to the valley below for a drink from the stream, and its absence of just a couple of seconds would give you time to discover the treasure hidden beneath!

The second walk is longer (about 12km), and visits a cross in the forest marking *la Fontaine des Agonisants* (Fountain of the Dying). This is a region with a wealth of wayside crosses – many were placed beside the pilgrim's route to Mont St Michel, and others marked the place of an event or happening. They often became associated with some superstition or legend. The route of this walk then follows a Grande Randonnée along the crest of a hill and passes through fine woods of oak and chestnut before returning to St Germain. The Office du Tourisme in Fougères has details of these walks – the text is in French, but the waymarking is good.

Walks further afield in the region can be found in a folder entitled *les Sentiers du Pays Gallo*, available from Tourist Information for a modest sum. These are walks with no text, good maps, and good waymarking. For yet more routes, see the 'More Walks' section of Walk 1.

Places of interest nearby

The walk passes the *Parc Floral* in the gardens of the Château la Folletière. These lovely formal gardens are well worth a visit and are open every day from the beginning of March to mid-December.

If you are taking this walk at le Châtellier, you must, of course, visit Fougères, with its superb medieval castle, old town area and fine views from the public gardens above. And the whole region is full of history and legend – again, see Walk 1.

3. Around the Pointe du Grouin

East of St Malo, the rocky finger of the Pointe du Grouin guards the entrance to the bay of Mont St Michel. A coastal path winds around the cliffs to reach its rugged tip, where there are fine views of the coastline from Cotentin to Cap Fréhel.

Grade: Moderate. Not suitable for young children as the paths are narrow and run along steep cliffs.

Distance: 6km (3¾ miles)

Time: 2 hours, including time at the Point

Map: IGN Top 25 1116 ET or Top 25 1215 OT

Start and finish: The sea front at Port-Mer

How to get there: Cancale is 14km east of St Malo. From Cancale, head north towards Pointe du Grouin, turning right after 3km (S.P. Port-Mer). There is parking along the sea front.

Refreshments: There are various bar/restaurants along the sea-front at Port-Mer. Cancale can apparently offer you a selection of about 50. There is also a restaurant at the Pointe du Grouin, open in summer.

Notes: This short walk is on good paths, quite suitable for trainers. But you might need a head for heights and children should be watched very closely. Take binoculars for the view from the Point (although there are telescopes) and beachwear if you intend to spend time at the Plage des Saussayes or at Port-Mer.

Waymarking: The coastal path here is the GR34 and therefore has white on red waymarks. There are no waymarks on the short road section on the return.

Introduction

There is an old saying that the tide comes in across St Michael's Bay faster than a horse can gallop. Perhaps it was originally meant as a warning to wandering equestrians but it nevertheless creates a dramatic picture of what happens here. At high tide, there is a bay of sparkling blue water; at low tide there are grey mudflats as far as the eye can see, broken only by the posts where mussels are cultivated and the dark rectangular oyster beds. The region for mussel farming is in the south of the bay near le-Vivier-sur-Mer, while Cancale, just below the Pointe du Grouin is the centre for oysters – although the young ones, the spats, are actually imported from near Auray in the Gulf of Morbihan and only 'grown on' here

Cancale is a fascinating place. Below the main town is the port area where you can watch the comings and goings of the oyster farmers at low tide and survey the plethora of stalls laden with gnarled crustaceans. The air smells of salt and iodine and fish, and chippings of more shells scrunch beneath your feet. Oysters, it seems, are not simply oysters – there are bélons and creuses and pieds de cheval, the latter

Pointe du Grouin

being huge and very expensive. If you are not a do-it-yourself oyster-eater, the town sports a mere fifty or so restaurants that will serve you with the delicacy – although, surprisingly, the prices here are often as high as you might find in Paris.

There is a good coastal path all the way from Cancale to the Pointe du Grouin, but in order to provide a circular walk, this route starts from Port-Mer, a very pretty little village up the coast. Port-Mer has no port, but boasts a fine sandy bay between rocky headlands – and, of course, a few restaurants serving oysters. The path from here is a Grande Randonnée that hugs the cliff-face all the way and has fine views across the bay. Before you reach the Point, there is a restaurant and parking area – with the result that, at least in summer, you are unlikely to have the place to yourself. Farther along comes a signalling station, and then the Point itself, a long, rocky promontory of wild moorland, some 40 metres above the sea. Beside it is the Île des Landes, a long bare outcrop now a bird sanctuary, and beyond this, a lighthouse clings to yet another rock. On a clear day, the views are superb and there is a toposcope to help you pick out the various features. Out to sea are the Îles Chaussey, farther over is Granville on the Normandy coast, and behind is the bay, across which can be seen the well-known outline of Mont St Michel.

On the west side of the Point is the Brittany coast, sweeping in rocky curves past St Malo to Cap Fréhel. On this side, the path is at times even more precarious as it threads its way along steep slopes of gorse and bracken high above the sea. Arriving at civilisation in the form of another sandy beach, it is time to return to Port-Mer. This short – but exhilarating – walk should leave you with plenty of time to try out the oysters.

The Walk

1. Walk along the promenade heading north (sea on the right), and at its end, begin the climb uphill on the tarmacked road. Very soon the white on red waymarkings of the Grande Randonnée are directing you to turn right on to a little path running around the cliffside. As you go you will notice several World War II German blockhouses set in the rock beside the path –some are now used as bird-watching hides. The path leads out to a headland known as the Pointe de Barbe Brulée, from which there are good views out into the bay. Ahead of you the Pointe de Grouin can now be seen, and beside it, the tip of the Île des Landes. Continuing from here, the path skirts a camping site and continues through the gorse and bracken alongside the Vieille Rivière, the channel between mainland and island. Keep ahead below the old signalling station to reach paths leading to the Point itself. The whole area is a nature reserve and you are asked to keep to these paths to reduce erosion and preserve the delicate vegetation.

2. The toposcope close to the tip will give you an idea of what can be seen from here. If the day is reasonable, you should at least be able to pick out the Îles Chaussey off the Normandy coast, Granville on its headland opposite, and Mont Dol and Mont St Michel across the bay.

   When you are ready to return, walk back past the signalling station and again pick up the GR as it leaves the car parking area. The path now runs along the west side where rough moorland covers steep slopes down to the sea. Ahead of you, the point of land is the Pointe du Meinga before St Malo, and beyond it you can see Cap Fréhel, some 35km away 'as the crow flies'. The path is easy to follow, and at one time, comes up to join the road for a few metres, before descending again into the bracken. At length you arrive above a sandy beach, the Plage des Saussayes.

3. Do not go down to the beach, but instead, bear left uphill to pass a car park and reach the road. Cross this road and continue down the Rue des Tintiaux opposite. From here, turn left into the Rue de la Vieille Rivière, and then cross the main road directly to head downhill to the beach at Port-Mer.

More Walks in the Area

This walk has given you just a taste of the GR 34, the coastal path that runs along the north coast of Brittany to Finistère. That may be a bit far

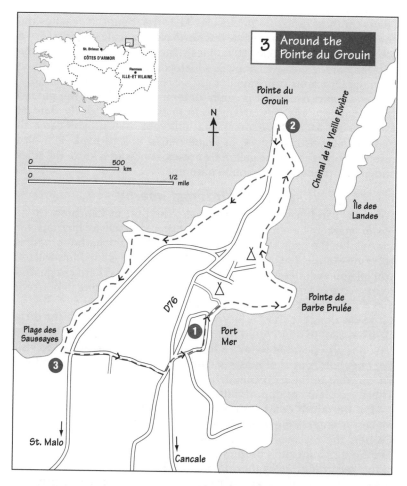

for you (it's about 300 miles!), but consider just the section from Pointe du Grouin to St Malo, a distance of about 24km. This really is a most attractive coastline, with opportunities for swimming and plenty of interesting places to visit en route – see Rothéneuf below. Moreover, the whole route is covered by a summer bus service between Cancale and St Malo. It is perfect for walkers! Enquire at the Office du Tourisme in Cancale.

Of course, the GR continues also in the opposite direction along the shores of the bay towards Mont St Michel. Le-Vivier-sur-Mer (a very interesting place – see below) is about 15km away, but sadly there is no direct bus route and you will need a taxi.

For another circular walk, you could return to the Plage des Saussayes and follow the north coast along to the Plage du Guesclin. Opposite the fort here, another Grande Randonnée, the GR 34a, heads south to cross the peninsula. At Terrelabouët, it reaches the coast again, and you can follow this north past Cancale to Port-Mer – a round trip of about 17km (10½ miles). These GRs are marked on the IGN map of the area (see above), which you should be able to obtain from the Office du Tourisme in Cancale, or any newsagent's shop.

For an excursion that is really different, join one of the guided walks out into the bay arranged from the Maison de la Baie at le-Vivier-sur-Mer. There are several different routes – you can visit beds of mussels or oysters, or wade out to a sand bank or a bird reserve. Forget about the galloping horses – the guides know the tides and also carry radio and mobile phones.

Places of interest nearby

You must surely visit Port de la Houle, the port of Cancale with its oyster market – even if you cannot bring yourself to buy any for supper. On the edge of the town (continue along the harbour road) is la Ferme Marine, the oyster museum. Here, displays and films will tell you all you ever need to know about *ostréiculture*. There are guided tours, some of which are in English, possibilities of tasting (if booked) and a shop full of oyster memorabilia.

15km along the coast is le-Vivier-sur-Mer, where the Maison de la Baie has a lot to offer. Apart from the already mentioned walks in the bay, it is also possible to take a train ride out on the mudflats to visit the *bouchots* (posts) of mussels. The mussels here have an excellent flavour due to the high concentration of plankton in the bay water. There are plenty of opportunities to sample them.

On the north coast, towards St Malo, the village of Rothéneuf makes an interesting visit. Here, in the 16th century, lived Jacques Cartier, the discoverer of Canada. His now restored house – the Manoir de Limoëlou – is open to the public and you can see charts, video recordings and other details of his voyages. The village also boasts some extraordinary rock carvings, made by a retired priest in the late 1800s, the Rochers Sculptés. There are more than 300 carvings of bizarre monsters and rather surrealistic figures on the cliff-face, high above an azure sea.

4. Locks on the canal at Hédé

The Ille-et-Rance Canal cuts through from Brittany's north coast to join the River Vilaine at Rennes – a very popular route for pleasure boaters. Near Hédé the canal climbs through beech woods, eleven locks leading up to its summit section beside an attractive lake

Grade: Easy – but a little tricky negotiating the banks of the feeder channel.

Distance: 6km (3¾ miles).

Time: 1½ hours

Map: IGN Série Bleue 1217 O – but get a print-out from the Maison Du Canal.

Start and finish: Maison du Canal d'Ille et Rance, la Magdeleine, Hédé

How to get there: Hédé is just off the D137, 20km north of Rennes. To get to la Magdeleine, leave Hédé by the Route de Combourg. In about 1km this road crosses the canal at la Magdeleine. The Maison du Canal is on the right, and there is parking on both sides of the canal.

Refreshment: There is a good bar/restaurant beside the Maison du Canal. There is also a small bar that serves snacks at Bazouges. Picnic tables are provided at the start (and finish) beside the canal.

Notes: This is a very short and easy walk along good tracks. The only problem is the crossing of the feeder channel from the lake – the banks of this are somewhat eroded and need care. It is said they are awaiting improvement.

Waymarking: Not much is needed since you are following canal, lake shore or road for most of the way. The path between canal and lake is waymarked in blue.

Introduction

A mere 20km separates the upper valley of the Rance from that of the Ille. It should have been a simple matter to connect the two – in fact it took more than 25 years and at one time, more than 1500 workers were employed on the task. In all, 85km of canal were created and 49 locks were needed between the barrage at Dinard and the city of Rennes. The canal had originally been a concept of Napoleon, a means of protecting his merchant fleet on the journey from the channel to the Bay of Biscay – from Rennes the journey was completed along the navigable River Vilaine. Napoleon and his troubles were long gone when the canal was finished in 1832.

The canal was in commercial use for over a century, but more recently it has become the preserve of the pleasure boaters – and very popular it is, too. One of the best places for seeing the action is here at la Magdeleine, near Hédé, where eleven locks take the canal up 27 metres to its summit level, the watershed between the Rance and the Ille. Each lock is accompanied by an old *maison d'éclusier* – a lock keeper's house. Narrowboats and barges of all sizes travel these waters in the summer months and you can have much fun as a gongoozler, a very English boater's term for those who stand by watching a boat working through a lock – there must be a French equivalent! At the end of the season, things are much quieter, but the canal here runs through beech woods making an autumn walk pure joy with its glorious colours.

At 65 metres, the summit is not very high, but those huge locks take away a lot of water each time a boat passes. A large lake was created at Bazouges to maintain the water level, and this has become naturalised and more attractive over the years. After setting out along the towpath, this walk leads you around the shores of this lake, which is a haven for wildfowl – as it is for French holiday makers. At the village of Bazouges-sous-Hédé you leave the lake and return on quiet roads to the Maison du Canal d'Ille et Rance – itself an old lock-keeper's house, which has become an eco-muséum with displays and information. And if the antics of the boaters have given you ideas of a holiday on water, this is the place to sort out the details!

Traditional barge on the Ille et Rance Canal, la Magdeleine

The Walk

1. From the Maison du Canal, walk uphill on the grassy towpath beside the canal (canal on your right). Huge oaks shade the path, with beech on the other side. At the first road bridge, cross over the canal and keep to the wide path under the beeches on the opposite bank. The path continues above the canal with a good view of events in the locks as you go. The Grande Randonnée (GR 37) joins you on this path, and white on red flashes are seen on the trees. At the next bridge, again cross the canal, and take the towpath now on its left-hand side. After following the canal for about 600 metres from this last bridge, just after a wooden house on the left, a blue arrow on a tree directs you off to the left.

2. Turn left following this arrow and keep to the path through the trees. Soon the path reaches the edge of the feeder channel coming from the lake. Turn left alongside the channel and cross it on the little bridge, working your way back along and above the

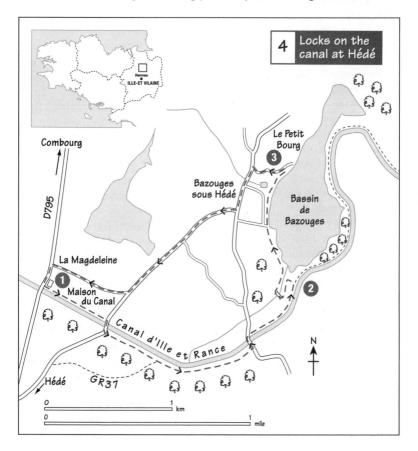

channel on the other side. The path from here is obvious, and soon becomes a wide track that passes some holiday homes beside the lake. At the junction, do not take the road on the left, but continue along the lake shore on the right. Keep beside this as far as the buildings of le Petit Bourg – about 15 minutes.

After passing some lakeside seats and crossing a little bridge and channel, leave the waterside between two old ivy-covered barns and cross the wooden planks over the ditch to reach a small road

3. Turn left on this road and continue to Bazouges-sous-Hédé. The road comes out beside the church. Now turn left down the main road, and after about 200 metres, take the right turn sign-posted to Hédé. After keeping to this road for something just over a kilometre, take a road on the right signed to la Magdeleine. A further few minutes walking will bring you to a T-junction, where you turn left on the main road. Just ahead is the canalside scene at la Magdeleine – boats, locks, picnic tables, bar/restaurant and eco-museum – all waiting to claim your attention.

More Walks in the Area

The Maison du Canal produces a photocopied map on which four circuits have been marked. This walk approximates to one of them. Two of the others follow the water channel up to Hédé – a town which itself is well worth visiting. One route then continues on the GR 37 to St Symphorien, an interesting village with an ancient manor facing a fine 16th century church and returns on a path beside the *fontaine de l'Ecuellée*, a site of pilgrimage. The other route sweeps east from Hédé passing some prehistoric standing stones before returning to the canal banks. Both routes are about 12km in length. A certain amount of French is necessary to follow the descriptions, but it should be possible to get around the routes using map alone. Unfortunately, there is no waymarking.

The Maison du Canal has leaflets of several other walks in the area from a series (in French) called *Petites Promenades en Bretagne Romantique*. The routes have good sketch maps, but it does seem that waymarking is, literally, thin on the ground around here. The walk at Tinténiac, 5km north, is neatly divided into two linked circuits of 4 and 5km These should be quite easy to follow from map alone as they are almost entirely on canal towpath or small road.

A couple of kilometres farther north at Québriac, two further circuits in this series are described. One is a canalside route (6.5km), while the other, a mere 3km, starts from a mill in an attractive wooded site beside the river. A longer circuit can be made by linking the two – call at the Mairie (Town Hall) for details.

In all, there are more than 20 leaflets in this series, so there is plenty of scope for excursions. But if you are not fairly fluent in French, a sense of adventure will be needed to tackle them.

Unfortunately, the towpath of the Ille-et-Rance Canal is not in perfect condition all the way. But if you walk east from the Maison du Canal (or from Hédé itself), you have about 12km of easy walking as you are on the route of the GR 37 all the way. There are picnic tables at la Plousière (7km) and full restaurant facilities further on at Montreuil-sur-Ille. To reach this town, leave the canal at the Écluse de Langagé (this is the third lock going downhill), cross over the bridge and continue along the road for about 1km. Montreuil also has a bus service which connects with Hédé, so you could make this a one-way trip in either direction. Details are available from the Office du Tourisme in Tinténiac (there is no Office du Tourisme in Hédé) – which regrettably is open only in summer.

Places of interest nearby

The village of Hédé stands on a hill above the canal and is itself worth a visit. It is a watery place, having also a large lake on its opposite side, and streams tumbling down in all directions. The crumbling houses and castle ruins are masked by the wealth of vegetation, and prolific hanging terraces cling to the hillside. All is topped by a Romanesque church, which can be seen for miles around.

Just 5km away by road or canal is Tinténiac, another small town in a picturesque setting. Beside the canal stands an old wooden grain house which is now the home of the Musée d'Outil et des Métiers – a museum of tools and trades with displays of workplaces such as a blacksmith's forge and a shoemaker's shop, all in working order.

If you enjoy castles, there are plenty in this area. The Château de Montmuran, 4km west, is a medieval castle with moat and drawbridge and high towers that can be climbed for the view. Continuing west, just through Bécherel is the Château de Caradeuc, this time a fine Regency-style château whose park and landscaped gardens are open to the public. And the castle to beat all castles is the grey, turreted, pepperpot-roofed, feudal fortress at Combourg. Built in the 11th century, it was once owned by du Guesclin, but is most famous as the childhood home (albeit for only two years) of the Romantic author François-René Chateaubriand. He later wrote so evocatively about his austere life there and his room in the haunted 'Cat Tower' that a visit to these places has become a necessary pilgrimage for those who wish to understand his later work.

5. The Megaliths of St Just

This is an excellent walk in the upper valley of the River Vilaine. Pine woods, gorse and heather, old villages, a lake, and fine distant views all come before the moorland of Cojoux, where a surprisingly diverse assortment of megaliths is scattered over a wide area.

Grade: Moderate with short strenuous section.

Distance: 13km (8 miles) A short cut can reduce this to about 10km.

Time: 3½ hours for the full walk – but you will want time to look at the megaliths.

Map: IGN Série Bleue 1120 E and 1120 O

Start and Finish: The church at St Just

How to get there: From Redon, take the D177 north towards Rennes. After 19km, turn left where sign-posted to St Just. Keeping ahead, the church is on the right-hand side of the road, and there is a large car park in front of it.

Refreshment: There is a bar/restaurant in St Just, but no other refreshment en route.

Notes: Walking boots are required, except perhaps in dry weather in summer. The walk is actually only strenuous on the path beside the lake (clambering over rocks) and the subsequent climb to the moors. With no refreshment available en route, it is advisable to carry fluid in warm weather – and you might like to take your binoculars for the views. The short cut from Point 3 to le Vieux Bourg will cut out about 3km, but the section missed is particularly attractive. For more details of the megaliths and the flora and fauna of the *landes*, equip yourself with a leaflet (in French) obtainable from the *Mairie* in St Just before you leave.

Waymarking: Over half the walk is on the GR 39 with white on red waymarks. The centre section has been waymarked in both blue and yellow.

Introduction

The megalithic site at St Just has been classified as the second such site in Brittany – and it is mercifully without the crowds found at Carnac. The collection here is quite amazing – menhirs, allées couvertes (gallery graves), barrows, dolmens, and alignments are sprinkled liberally in a landscape of gorse, broom and heather on land known as the Grée de Cojoux. Being Brittany, many of the megaliths have legends attached to them. The Three Demoiselles, three huge menhirs, are said to be three maidens turned to stone because they went to play on the moors rather than attend vespers. The Chateau-Bû, a huge dolmen with chambers and corridors, is rather more sinister – it is said that a young virgin was sacrificed here every year. Fortunately, this is almost certainly mythical! At the Croix de St Pierre, an ancient

Alignments and old mill at St Just

cross-roads, there are several dolmens and tumuli, and here were found two vases dating from about 5000BC. Perhaps most amazing of all, although not quite so impressive to look at, is a semi-circle of rocks known as the Tribunal – it is actually a prehistoric calendar. The rocks mark the points at which the sun rises and sets at different times of the year when viewed from one distant rock. The tallest rock of all marks the point of sunset at the winter solstice.

A short walk from St Just will take you out to all these megaliths. But if you have more time to spare, the route described here is well worth taking as it is as varied and scenic in a gentle sort of way as any you will find in Brittany. There are many turns and junctions as the well-waymarked paths lead you over moorland, through woodland, past tiny hamlets of granite-grey houses, up hills with fine views and into remote valleys with babbling streams. Eventually you arrive beside a most attractive lake in a deep valley and follow its shores for some distance, scaling a few rocky outcrops as you go. A steep climb to the moorland summit follows, and you are on the Grée de Cojoux. Grée is an old Breton word meaning 'height' – and so it is. Wild, wind-swept and mysterious, dotted with gorse and heather, this is a perfect setting for a remarkable prehistoric exhibition. What spurred the ancients to mark this place with every monument they knew? How closely are these megaliths related in time? You can ponder these questions and many others all the way back to St Just.

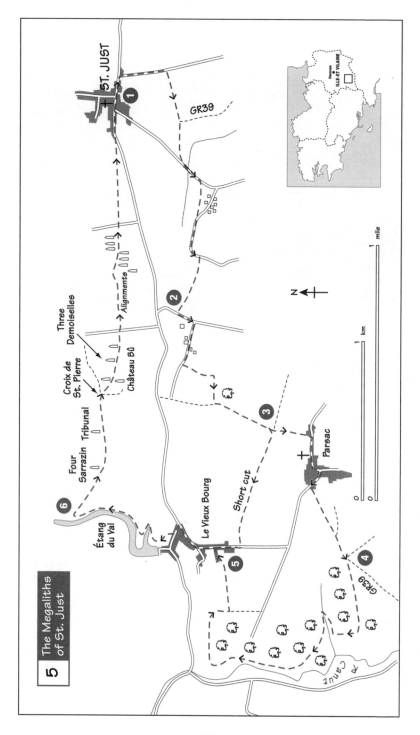

5 The Megaliths of St. Just

The Walk

1. With the church behind you, walk down to the main road and turn left (following the D54 in the direction of St Ganton) At the cross-roads in about 150 metres, turn right, following the white on red waymarks of the Grande Randonnée.

   In a further 250 metres or so, the waymarks direct you to turn right on a pleasant stony track through pines and gorse. In a few minutes you reach a track junction where the GR leaves to turn left beside the pines. Your route lies straight ahead, now following blue waymarks down the stony track to reach a tarmacked road. Here turn left, cross the bridge over a stream, and in about 150 metres, look for a grassy track on the right. Following this, a farm is passed on the left, and you continue ahead. Soon the track corners sharply left, and just after this, you turn right (fortunately all this is well-waymarked – in both blue and yellow) and then keep ahead to meet a narrow tarmacked road.

2. Turn left on this road. Passing a big old granite farmhouse, immediately turn right and continue for about 250 metres. The waymarks now lead left on to a grassy and stony track climbing uphill. Nearing the top of the hill, turn right and continue climbing towards a spinney on the summit. At the track junction, turn left and skirt the woods on a track from which there are now wide views of the moorland to the north. The track descends to a cross-roads, and now you have a choice.

3. If you wish to take a short cut, turn right here and follow the track for almost a kilometre, finally turning right at the road to reach the village of le Vieux Bourg. Here the longer route joins you from the left (Point 5) and you walk through the village, picking up the white on red marks of the GR again.

   To continue with the main route, cross straight over at the track junction following blue and yellow waymarks. On reaching a farm, you turn right on the tarmacked road and continue on the waymarked route through the beautiful old granite houses of Parsac. At the end of the village, the road forks, but you want an open yard on the left beside a quarry. From this yard there are two tracks – take the left-hand one, which again is waymarked. This soon leads down through a pretty wooded valley beside a stream and eventually you arrive at a wide curving stony track where you continue ahead. A further 100 metres or so brings you to a track junction.

4. Bear right at this junction. The GR39 has arrived from the left and its white on red waymarks now join the blues and yellows to guide you all the way back to St Just. The next stretch is most attractive as the path follows the woodland edge and finally arrives in a pretty

valley where a river (the Canut) gurgles below you on the left. After passing stepping stones and a ford in the river, the path turns and climbs through the wood again. At the crown of the hill, the path winds around a field, and then turns sharply left to descend to le Vieux Bourg.

5. On reaching the tarmacked road, turn left and continue through the village. You might almost think le Vieux Bourg aptly named as there seem so many derelict properties here. Just before the road junction, an old *four à pain* (bread oven) stands long redundant beside the road. At the junction, turn left and continue on this road for about 50 metres, to reach a small car park on the right. It seems a strange place for a car park, but the reason is soon obvious as you follow the GR up the hill behind it. The path leads on to the *landes de Cojoux* and below you the *Étang du Val* sparkles in its rocky wooded valley. The GR marks guide you through the moorland and take you down to the lakeside. Following the bank of the lake, you cross entrant streams on two bridges. Continue now beside the lake for a further 15 minutes or so, climbing over various rocky outcrops.

6. Suddenly the path doubles back, leaving the lake and climbing quite steeply to reach the moorland above. Here there are fantastic views in all directions. The path bears left and soon, on the left, you see the Four Sarrazin (a tumulus surmounted by an allée couverte) and this is followed by the rocks of the Tribunal. Next comes the Croix de St-Pierre, then the Chateau-Bû, the Demoiselles and finally the alignments – those beside your path running east-west, others running north-south. This dramatic display of prehistory comes right at the end of the walk, so you can afford to take time over it. From here, it is but 10 minutes walk back to St Just – cross over the road at the end, and follow the footpath across the field opposite. This brings you to the road at the entrance to the village, and you have only to turn left along it to return to the church.

More Walks in the Area

The moorland of Cojoux lies between the valleys of the River Vilaine and the River Oust. The GR39, which you meet on this walk, follows the course of the River Vilaine between Rennes and the sea at Pénestin. A Topoguide, *Vallée de la Vilaine et de l'Oust (Ref. 077)*, describes the route of the GR39 as well as giving 50 circular walks in the area. This Topoguide can be obtained from any bookshop or Office du Tourisme, but unfortunately is published only in French. This should not be too great a problem as maps and waymarking are clear. Two nearby walks from this Topoguide make particularly good excursions.

The first is from Renac, just a few kilometres south of St Just. Here there is a long (18km) route, which is waymarked in blue and designated as suitable for both walkers and mountain bikers (VTT). Again largely taking the route of the GR39, it wanders around this most attractive countryside, first following the valley of the River Canut with water mills and an old chapel. It then sets off across wooded slopes and moorland, passing a fine château and an ancient hamlet of granite houses with enclosures of granite slabs.

The second walk is rather different. About 7km east of St Just, a waymarked route starts from the Pont St-Marc, the bridge over the River Vilaine on the D 53. This is a short circuit of 6km, which passes through attractive woodland (the Bois de Boeuvres), follows the towpath of the Vilaine and visits an old hermit's cave with a view. Tourist Information at Messac should have details.

The River Vilaine is joined to the Canal d'Ille-et-Rance, making a navigable waterway cutting right across Brittany from Dinan in the north to la Roche Bernard in the south. A towpath follows the route much of the way, giving excellent possibilities for walking.

The *Pays d'Accueil Touristique de Vilaine* produces a hard-backed file entitled *Les Sentiers de la Rando*. This file contains brightly-coloured cards describing waymarked walks in 18 locations in the vicinity of Redon. All these walks rely on maps and excellent waymarking – the short French text with each merely adds a few points of interest. The publication can be obtained from the Office du Tourisme in Redon and other locations. Interesting circuits are described at La Chapelle de Brain, 8km south of St Just (river and marais) and Sixt-sur-Aff, about the same distance to the west (hills and woodland).

Places of interest nearby

If you have developed a taste for megaliths, the other most interesting site in the area is at Monteneuf, about 30km north-east, on the D776 from Malestroit to Guer. For many years, only four menhirs were visible here. Observations on the area revealed that, in fact, there were over 400 of these stones scattered over 7 hectares. They are now in process of being re-erected. The site is said to be between four and six thousand years old, and was probably standing until about a thousand years ago when religious orders demanded its destruction. Excavations go on each summer and there is an exhibition and guided tours. There is also a very interesting waymarked circuit of 14km visiting other archaeological sites in the area.

The villages of Caro and la Chapelle Caro (between Malestroit and Ploërmel) both have interesting megalithic remains. At Caro there are two allées couvertes while at la Chapelle Caro there is an allée couverte and a dolmen (le Dolmen de la Maison Trouée) which is of the 'Angevin' type, more recent than the classical dolmens (Dolmens à couloir)

Getting into more modern history, at St Marcel, just west of Malestroit, there is the fascinating Musée de la Resistance, chronicling local life and Breton resistance in the last war. Army vehicles and the like are set out in a park of six hectares, around which you can be driven in an American military wagon.

Rather closer to St Just, the town of Redon (19km south) is worth a visit. It is a watery place – here both River Vilaine and River Oust meet the Nantes à Brest Canal, and pleasure cruisers are heading in all directions. You can wander beside the canals enjoying the antics of the boaters in the locks, or even take to the water yourself on one of the cruisers that go up or down the Vilaine.

For something different, the town of la Gacilly, about 15km west of St Just, is the home of the large Yves Rocher perfume factory. You can visit their museum – and, of course, make purchases.

6. Brocéliande – The Val sans Retour

On the map you will see the Forest of Paimpont – it is in your imagination that you will find Brocéliande, the mythical home of King Arthur and the Knights of the Round Table. The forest is teeming with legendary sites and stories of their exploits. This walk is through a beautiful valley on which a spell has been cast by the fairy Morgane – beware!

Grade: Moderate

Distance: 5km (3 miles)

Time: 1½ hours

Map: IGN Série Bleue 1019 E

Start and Finish: The church at Tréhorenteuc

How to get there: Tréhorenteuc is north-east of Ploërmel – follow the D141for about 13km It is on the western edge of the forest. There is a large new parking area in the village, close to the church.

Refreshment: There is a pleasant bar/restaurant in Tréhorenteuc.

Notes: This is just a short walk, but if you feel energetic, you can combine it with one of the two walks mentioned below. All the forest information offices have details. Shoes or trainers would be suitable for this walk in summer, but in winter the paths can be quite boggy, requiring more substantial footwear.

Waymarking: From Tréhorenteuc to the head of the valley, you are following the GR 37 with its white on red waymarks. The return path is waymarked with yellow flashes.

Introduction

The stories of King Arthur and the Knights of the Round Table are well-known on both sides of the channel. Having their roots in Celtic mythology, they were 'Christanised' and brought to the people by the minstrels and troubadours of the Middle Ages. One of the most famous of these was Chrétien de Troyes, who told some of the earliest of the Arthurian tales in 12th century Brittany. Forests were always places of legend and enchantment, and these stories became located here – the Forest of Paimpont became Brocéliande. It was to this place, they said, that Joseph of Arimathea brought the Holy Grail, the cup from which Christ drank at the Last Supper, and in which he collected a few drops of Christ's blood after the Crucifixion. Here, Arthur and his Knights pursued that Holy Grail, but the forest itself has more connections with Merlin, magician at Arthur's court.

Merlin was the son of the Devil and a woman, and was friend, adviser and sorcerer to King Arthur. He lived not in the court, but in the forest itself, retiring there to meditate and weave spells. In the forest, you will find the fountain of youth from which he drank, and the magic fountain of Barenton beside which he met his eternally beloved fairy Viviane. Beneath the lake at Comper he built her a crystal palace and

In the forest of Brocéliande

his tomb is in a clearing in the woods. There are many, many legends associated with this forest. It is a beautiful place for walking in its own right, but only an incorrigible cynic would deny the sparkle these tales add to the scene.

This particular walk starts from the village of Tréhoronteuc in the west of the forest. In the middle of the twentieth century, the priest here was one Henri Gillard. He was so absorbed by the Arthurian legends that he began mingling Christianity and mythology in his church. The stained glass windows depict the disciples at the Last Supper – or are these the Knights of Arthur gathered at the round table? The Stations of the Cross have Arthurian themes, while Celtic mosaics and pictures of legendary creatures decorate the walls. Sadly for Gillard, his unorthodox ideas were not viewed favourably, and he was asked to leave. He was, however, loved by his parishioners and returned frequently, finally requesting to be buried in the church. This was granted – but how things have since changed! The church has become a place of curiosity, attracting many visitors to the little village. A tourist office is located opposite and organises conducted tours in summer. Visit out of season and you can have the key and explore for yourself. Most incredibly, a statue of the Rev. Gillard has been erected in front of the main door – he would have been amazed.

Leaving Tréhorenteuc, you head for the Valley of no Return, and it truly is one of the most beautiful parts of the forest. The story here is that the wicked fairy Morgane, the half-sister of King Arthur, was betrayed in love, and in revenge, imprisoned all faithless lovers in this valley, the steep sides of which prevented their escape. They were condemned to wander for ever in this place, whose entrance and exit were guarded by a rock (Rocher des Faux-Amants) on which sat the fairy herself. Think well before you take this walk! But if you feel you can risk it, there are fine rewards. Deep in the valley is a calm lake, the *Miroir aux Fées*, at which the fairy folk come to view their perfect reflections. Farther on is a smaller version of this lake with the path climbing high above its shores. A recent addition to the valley is the *Arbre d'Or* (Tree of Gold), a remarkable sculpture commissioned to commemorate the fire of 1990, which destroyed much of the forest – this valley was replanted by the Association for the Protection of the Val sans Retour. The return is along the rim of the valley with fine views into its deep bowl. Here Merlin would sit at sunset, watching the long shadows creep across the forest – walking here, perhaps you also can feel the magic of this place.

The Walk

1. Standing in the square in front of the church, face the church door and turn right on to the road, where you again go right (on the road to Campénéac). Leaving the village, you pass on the left an ancient half-timbered manor house. Just past the manor house is a large sign directing you left to the Val sans Retour. Now climb up the broad stony track with increasing views as you go. Reaching a barrier ahead, turn right on a track which is a fire-break and continue to the left-hand bend.

2. Here turn right on a track through the trees – it is waymarked with the white on red flashes of the Grande Randonnée. Following these waymarks, you reach a rocky edge amid gorse and heather, where the path begins to dip steeply into the valley. There are fine views over the lovely Miroir aux Fées as you descend. On crossing the bridge, the Arbre d'Or, is on your right. The sculptor is one François Davin, and he again used the Christian-mythological symbol of antlers as a design for a golden tree amid the black – life arising from the flames. On the left of the lake beside the path, once stood the old Moulin de la Vallée that was abandoned in 1930. Continuing, the path leads you around the end of the Miroir aux Fees – the Rocher des Faux-Amants is the red rock high on the left above the lake. Bear left on the path around the lake to enter the valley. Now keep ahead on the obvious path on the right of the stream (Ruisseau du Rauco), deep in the valley. On the way, you pass two dykes, which were at one time used to hold back the stream water. After about 15 minutes, you reach a wooden bridge at the end of a second lake – the site of a third dyke, which was restored by the association for the preservation of the valley.

3. The waymarks direct you to cross this bridge, and continue on the path, which now weaves its way through gorse and pines high above the lake on its far side. Soon it descends again, and crossing

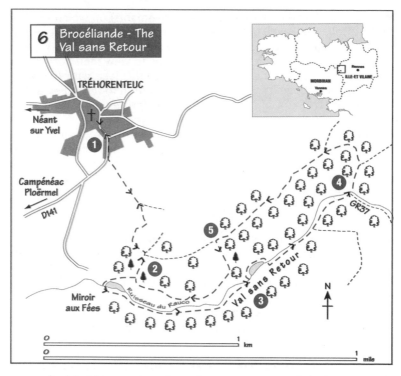

a plank bridge, you now have the stream on your left once more. A signpost shortly appears, and you follow the direction of *la Vallée de l'Aff,* straight on up beside the stream.

4. At a track junction (about 20 minutes from the last lake), the GR37 goes to the right, but you bear left following the yellow waymarks. Cross the stream, and continue to follow the yellow flashes along-side another stream. Bear left again on a track that now climbs out of the valley and rejoins the fire-break. Soon the track levels out and you are above the valley with distant views. Do not relax and think you are going to coast home from here.

5. As soon as the view opens out, look for an orange-flashed rock on the left. Take the path beside it, which heads through the gorse and the pines and threads its way around to come out along the very rim of the valley. The waymarks make an infrequent appear-ance at first, but continuing along the edge, you soon arrive at a reasonable track in the right direction. There are fine viewpoints back into the valley, one of which is Merlin's seat. Yellow flashes again appear and lead you across a surface of ridged rock and past another huge boulder to arrive at the GR you started out on ear-lier. Now turn right, and retrace your steps to the fire-break road, where you turn left to return to Tréhorenteuc.

More Walks in the Area

There are many fine walks in Brocéliande, and you should be able to get a map of the forest from tourist information in Paimpont, in Plélan-le-Grand or in Tréhorenteuc. In all, 21 circuits have been waymarked, each one having some particular point of interest – almost always, there is a legend attached to add to the fun. All the circuits are described in a Topoguide entirely devoted to the forest, *Tour de Brocéliande (Ref. 062)*. This Topoguide also has *idées rando* – suggestions for exploring the whole forest in three separate two-day circuits of about 45km With each of these there are proposed overnight stopping places – any Office du Tourisme would be prepared to help with booking accommodation.

Returning to circular walks, there are two circuits that could be combined with this one in the Val sans Retour to give a longer walk, or indeed take independently. Both are full of interest.

The first is a route entitled *les Landes de Gurwant* – 10km in length, it passes the superb Château de Trécesson. Built in red schist, and overlooking a lake, it is the most beautiful of the castles of Brocéliande. The path then continues past a huge megalith called the Giant's Tomb, and another 'coffin-shaped' prehistoric tomb known as the *Maison de Viviane*. This route connects with the Val sans Retour at the signpost after Point 3 and at Point 4, and so could also start at Tréhorenteuc.

The second is a route that visits the *Jardin aux Moines* – the Monks' Garden. This is a curious flat rectangle, surrounded by blocks of stone in alternate colours. Dating from about 3000BC, its true purpose is unknown, but legend has it that a local lord took a monk hostage and then went hunting on All Saints Day. During vespers, a mighty storm broke, and later that day this rectangle was found – the whole hunt had been turned to stone. This is a circuit of 8km, which also starts from Tréhorenteuc. Note that this particular part of the forest is closed during the winter months - for hunting!

Three waymarked circuits (lengths 10, 10 and 22km) start from Paimpont in the south of the forest. Each of them visits the attractive lake known as the Étang du Pas du Houx. The longest circuit also passes les Forges de Paimpont, a village dating from the 17th century when iron foundries had been established in the forest. This latter route is unfortunately closed in winter.

There are more routes in the north of the forest mentioned under the next walk, Walk 7 from the Château de Comper. For more details of all these routes, any Office du Tourisme should be able to help.

Places of interest nearby

One place you must visit in Brocéliande is the Fontaine de Barenton, and it is something of an adventure as it is not well advertised. Drive about 3km north from Tréhorenteuc to the village of Folle Pensée, and just through this village, bear right to reach a small parking area where there is a signpost to Barenton. Several paths lead into the forest but you take the main one ahead. After that you are on your own – but it is only about 1 km. The Fontaine de Barenton is a spring of crystal-clear water, in which rising bubbles of nitrogen give the appearance of boiling. It is the early descriptions of this spring that confirm the location of the legends of Brocéliande in the Forest of Paimpont. Legend has it that it was at the stone slab beside this spring that Merlin first met his beloved fairy Viviane, and here that she imprisoned him in nine magic circles of air to keep him in the forest forever. It is also said that if, in drinking from the fountain, you accidentally spill water on that stone, a huge storm will arise immediately. This appears to be so well authenticated that even the established church attempted to use its powers in the drought of 1835. There seems to be no record of what happened next, but even so, you should be very careful if you take a drink! A recent Arthurian Congress is certainly claiming success.

Travelling on past Folle-Pensée and through Concoret will bring you to the Château de Comper. Here it was said, the fairy Viviane was born and here she raised Sir Lancelot in her crystal palace below the waters of the lake. Coming down to earth, there has been a castle on this site for about a thousand years – it has been sacked many times, burned down, destroyed and again rebuilt. The château now houses the *Centre de l'Imaginaire Arthurien*, offering exhibitions and audio-visual displays to help revive your memory of the Arthurian legends – see Walk 7.

At the heart of the forest is the little town of Paimpont with its ancient abbey beside a large glassy lake. It is, to say the least, photogenic. In summertime you can picnic beside the lake or take out a pedalo on its peaceful waters.

7. Brocéliande – The Château de Comper

Here is a second walk in the enchanted forest of Brocéliande, the home of the legendary court of King Arthur. This one starts from the fairy-tale Château de Comper, which now houses the Centre for Arthurian Imagination. Before you visit it, you could take this gentle stroll in the forest to give you a feel for its magic.

Grade: Easy

Distance: 10km (6¼ miles)

Time: 2½ hours

Map: IGN Série Bleue 1018 E

Start and finish: The Château de Comper

How to get there: Comper lies on the D31, 2km east of Concoret. It can be reached from Paimpont by travelling north on the D773, and turning right where signed after about 4km There is some parking in front of the Château, and roadside parking is possible with care.

Refreshment: There are bars and restaurants in Concoret. Light refreshments are available at the Château when open.

Notes: The first part of the walk is on a rather overgrown forest track. Do not be put off – it isn't all like this. Later, there are broad tracks with good open views. Trainers should be suitable in summer, but remember that forests are almost always muddy in winter. After about 1¾ hours you should reach Concoret where there is refreshment.

Waymarking: The route is waymarked in blue throughout

Introduction

In the forest of Paimpont, the Breton story-tellers of the Middle Ages located one of the most famous legends of all time – the forest became Brocéliande, the scene of the court of King Arthur and the Knights of the Round Table.. Even now, the woodland conceals many sites associated with those ancient legends.

The Château de Comper, the original dating from around 1100, was said to be the birthplace of the fairy Viviane, dearly beloved of the court magician, Merlin. Below the waters of the lake he built for her a crystal palace, and here, as the Lady of the Lake, she brought up Sir Lancelot, delivering him to the court of Arthur in his fifteenth year. Few people are allowed to see that crystal palace, and even then for no more than a second. If you want to find out if you will have this privilege, you will have to come in summer as the château is, unfortunately, closed out of season. In winter, all you will see from the entrance is a crumbling turret and an overgrown moat. But if you are here between April and September, you can walk through and see the now-restored castle set beside an enchanted lake with perfect reflections. The château now houses the *Centre de l'Imaginaire Arthurien* –

an exhibition of tableaux and videos that will acquaint you with the legends and their place in this forest.

While you are at Comper you might wish to take a walk in the neighbouring forest – this one will take you about 2½ hours, but you could always have lunch at the village of Concoret en route. The legends associated with this sector of the forest are not particularly Arthurian, but there are plenty of those to be found elsewhere, as you will learn from the exhibition in the château. The walk heads off through quite thick woodland and soon comes upon three huge boulders known as the three Roches de Trébran. Apparently, they dropped from the aprons of fairies on their way to build Mont St Michel. In the absence of any better explanation for their presence - - but they must have been pretty strong fairies! Farther into the forest, there is suddenly an abundance of tropical plants. In the last world war, this was the site of a German camp, whose commandant was a keen gardener and nature lover. He had his camp planted with rare specimens, many from conquered or allied countries – some have lived on here for over half a century. After passing Concoret, an attractive village with a fine church of purple granite schist, it is an easy return on clear tracks to reach the château with its legends. If you remember that the lake is only a mirage, with luck you will glimpse that crystal palace beneath!

The Chateau de Comper

The Walk

1. From the Château de Comper, follow the road downhill towards the lake. At the fork before the lake, you should turn left (S.P. Muel), and keep to this road for about 200 metres to a sharp right-hand corner. Here an obvious track goes off on the left. This is not for you. Seek instead another track on the left a few metres farther on – a much overgrown track through gorse and broom. It is marked by a faded blue flash on a telegraph pole. This narrow path continues uphill through the bushes for about 1km, finally arriving at a hard-surfaced clearing, the junction of several tracks.

2. Turn left downhill and follow the road for about 800 metres. After a right-hand bend, there is a barrier on the road ahead. Here turn left and follow the hard track downhill. Soon the track bears right, and almost immediately afterwards you see a blue arrow urging you to turn right. If you continue ahead for about 50 metres here, you come to the rocks known as Les Trois Roches de Trébran. They are hiding in the forest on the right. Now return to that blue arrow at the junction and follow its direction uphill. The concrete rectangle beside the junction is the remains of the swimming pool at the German camp. Continue uphill past the ruined buildings of the camp, where you can still see surviving vegetation obviously alien to the forest. After two cross-tracks, an arrow on a tree directs you left. Soon turn right to reach the camp entrance, and then left to the main road.

3. Cross straight over the road (S.P. la Feuvrais) First bear left, then at the fork, leave the tarmacked road, keeping right. After about 700 metres, bear right at a sort of T-junction and shortly arrive at a tarmacked road. Cross straight over and head uphill towards the pine wood. At the cross-tracks before the wood, turn sharp left and continue downhill with very pleasant views for about 10 minutes. Several tracks are crossed as you go, but your track keeps straight ahead towards the church at Concoret and is clearly waymarked. Cross a small tarmacked road, and on reaching a second, turn left (church spire now on right). At the cross-roads, turn right towards Concoret.

4. Arriving in Concoret, you have the church on your left. Turn left around the church wall and keep straight ahead, following signs to Comper and blue waymarks. About 250 metres from the church, there is a cross-roads, where you turn right. Soon this road itself bears to the left, but you continue ahead following the *Circuit de Comper* with its blue flashes. At a big cross-tracks with fine views to the right, turn left

5. At the tarmacked road (250 metres), turn left. After about 100 metres, turn right beside a house (there seem to be orange dots

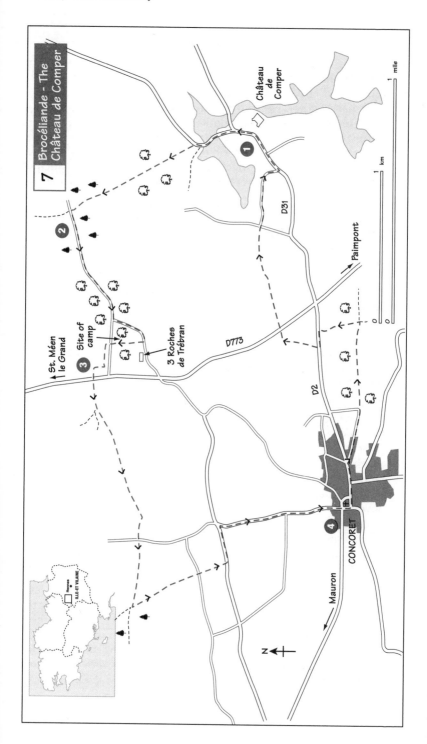

7 Brocéliande – The Château de Comper

Château de Comper

St. Méen le Grand

3 Site of camp

3 Roches de Trébran

D31

D773

D2

Paimpont

Mauron

CONCORET

ILLE-ET-VILAINE

1 km

1 mile

N

rather than blue here). Continuing ahead, the track turns sharp right and comes to a main road. Cross straight over to the broad earthy track opposite. At this point waymarks are unaccountably absent. After a track on the right is passed, you arrive at a track junction. Here you take the track bearing away to the right (a farm is seen in the distance ahead). After about 300 metres, cross a narrow tarmacked road and continue ahead past the farm. The road now bears right past other houses and farm buildings to reach a larger road. This is the D31 and here you turn left for about 250 metres to reach the Château de Comper.

More Walks in the Area

21 circuits are marked out in this forest, most of them having associations with legend or pre-history – or both. Of course, the forest is most attractive in its own right. Predominantly of oak and beech, it is at its most glorious in autumn colours. In the forest are many lakes – too many to count, it seems, as the guide books suggest anything from 14 to 35! One of the prettiest of these is the Étang du Pas du Houx in the south, and three waymarked circuits in all visit this – see under Walk 6. The forest is also known for its châteaux, and there are two beside this lake.

Merlin's Tomb is one of the important forest sites not too far from Comper – in fact, it is probably the remains of an ancient megalith. However, it would be a shame not to join in with the spirit of the place, and as well as the tomb, you can also visit the nearby Fontaine de Jouvence, from which Merlin drank to preserve his youth. Drinking is not strictly necessary! Apparently, if you gaze into the waters for just one minute, this should be sufficient to remove wrinkles – provided you have bare feet at the time. A 12km circuit starting from the village of St-Malon-sur-Mel passes these two sites along with an old stone quarry, an ancient menhir and an allée couverte known as the Tombeau des Anglais.

In the north of the forest are two attractive areas – the lake and woods of Trémelin and the Valley of the Chambre au Loup. Up here, they seem to be running out of Arthurian legends, but the countryside makes pleasant walking. The Val de la Chambre au Loup is quite dramatic, even if the local description of 'Grand Canyon' goes a bit far. Five routes are described in this part of the forest

And lastly, do not forget Walk 6 – the most beautiful Val sans Retour and the church with its legends at Tréhorenteuc. For maps of the forest and details of these circuits and others, any of the Offices du Tourisme in the area (Plélan-le-Grand, Paimpont, Tréhorenteuc) should be able to help

Places of interest nearby

The Château de Comper is well worth a visit. In addition to the exhibition, there is a bookshop with a wide range of publications. If you want to know more about the forest and its legends, you could look out for a short book published in several languages including English, and entitled *Brocéliande – Its High Places*. The Château is open on Mondays, Wednesdays and Thursdays in April, May and September, and every day except Tuesday in June, July and August. It is closed from October to March. Before going, it is probably best to check all this with Tourist Information.

The lake of Trémelin has a recreation area that will appeal to the young at heart. There is a small sandy beach for swimming; pedalos, canoes and other boats can be hired; there are facilities for mini-golf, badminton and tennis, and there is also an excellent bar/restaurant serving everything from take-aways and snacks to a five-course meal.

Paimpont at the heart of the forest is just a small town but is well worth a visit. Beside a beautiful lake is an abbey, formerly a monastery founded in 645 by the Breton King Judicaël. Of course, there is nothing of the original left, but the abbey church is 12th century, and quite stunning in its lakeside setting.

Further places of interest in the forest are described under Walk 6. You should not miss the Arthurian church at Tréhorenteuc, and follow it with a short walk to seek out the Fontaine de Barenton. If you wish to visit the Miroir aux Fées and the Arbre d'Or mentioned in Walk 6, you can actually get there by car, turning left off the road to Campénéac. But the mysteries of the Val sans Retour are for walkers alone.

Fishing fleet at Erquy

Côtes-d'Armor

8. Rocky shores at the Lac de Guerlédan

Set in wooded hills at the heart of Brittany, this lake has an almost alpine feel to it. Popular with French holiday makers – although not yet with British – it offers sailing, canoeing, swimming – and walking! This short ramble gives you just a taste of the many waymarked routes in the area.

Grade: Moderate (should be easy – but there are one or two scrambles over rocks beside the lake)

Distance: 6km (3¾ miles)

Time: 2 hours

Map: IGN Série Bleue 0818 E

Start and Finish: The Rond-Point of the Lac de Guerlédan, Mûr-de-Bretagne

How to get there: Mûr-de-Bretagne is just south of the N164 between Loudéac and Rostrenen. The Rond-Point is on the lake, 1km west of the town (follow signs to *Centre Nautique*). There is good parking at the Rond-Point.

Refreshment: There is an attractive bar/restaurant at the Rond-Point with views over the lake, and yet another bar on the approach road. Unfortunately, neither is open in winter. Mûr-de-Bretagne is a pleasant little town with good restaurant facilities of all kinds.

Notes: The walk should be quite suitable for trainers in dry weather in summer. At other times, walking boots are advised. There are no opportunities for refreshment en route, so you might like to carry water – but it is only a short walk.

The route is waymarked throughout – at first with the white and red bars of the Grande Randonnée and then with yellow flashes.

Introduction

Hurrying by on your way to the beaches of Finistère, you may just have glanced south from the busy N164 near Mûr-de-Bretagne and glimpsed a landscape of forested hills and deep valleys, and among them, the waters of the Lac de Guerlédan. The *Suisse Breton* is a term that the tourist board has used for this area – which is certainly overstepping the mark a little. Nevertheless, it is very attractive, and a far cry from what most British holidaymakers think of as a Breton landscape.

The Lac de Guerlédan is almost entirely surrounded by woodland that reaches to its shores and spills over the cliffs of grey granite schist. Surprisingly, this picturesque lake is man-made, formed some 60 years ago when the Blavet, like so many other French rivers, was dammed to provide hydro-electric power. The Blavet here was part of the Nantes to Brest Canal, a waterway created by Napoleon to bypass the attacks of the British fleet in the Bay of Biscay. This no longer being a problem, the canal has more recently been turned over to pleasure craft – but Guerlédan now effectively splits it in two, and boaters must content themselves with half a canal to east or west. The lake attracts a different kind of boating in its own right – in summer a medley of canoes, dinghies, windsurfers and trip-boats ply the waters.

The shores offer other attractions – you can hire a pedalo or play mini-golf, go for a swim or build sand castles on the beach. You can also take a walk! The woods around are laced with trails and circuits and indeed, a Grande Randonnée encircles the whole lake. Farther back, those wooded slopes are cut by gorges where rivers tumble in spectacular fashion to end in the waters of the lake or the River Blavet.

The walk chosen here is just a short one and follows the shores of the *Anse de Landroannec* at the eastern end. The lake is said to have the shape of a dragon from the air – in which case, you are walking around its head. The route first follows the Grande Randonnée beside the lake and through the Bois de Cornac – fine woods of beech, chestnut and oak along its shores. The return is an easy walk along the route of an old railway line with good views of the surrounding countryside. Back at the Rond-Point you can enjoy a meal overlooking the lake, or if you fancy a swim, take a 5-minute drive to the pretty beach at Caurel.

The Walk

1. Take the path that heads into the woods to the right of the *Basse Nautique* buildings. You will see the white on red bar markings of the Grande Randonnée on the trees. Continue up beside the fence and at the top bear left, and again to the left at the site board. Here is a fine view, but leave the rustic seat for your return. Try instead the *Parcours Sportif,* which runs alongside your path at this point. At the end of this, at a fork, bear downhill to the left towards the lake. Now continue on a very scenic path above and beside the lake, following the GR waymarks through woods of beech, oak and holly where occasional seats are placed to tempt you. Eventually the well-signed path leaves the shore and climbs up to a *Village de Vacances*.

2. At the tarmacked road, turn right and then immediately left to cross the car parking area. At the far side of this, beneath the electricity lines, a path leads down beside the field to reach the lake again. At the lakeside (there is a fine beach to the left), turn right and continue beside the lake with open views. At the first junction, beside some wooden buildings, turn left and keep ahead on the road, passing the end of the lake and a picnic site.

3. Leaving the lake, turn left at the T-junction. At the next junction, in about 400 metres, turn right away from the lake. This road junction is also a junction of Grandes Randonnées, the point where the main GR341 (which you are now going to follow) splits into

North and South versions to encircle the lake. After walking uphill for about 150 metres, turn right on to the gravelly track of an old railway, again marked with white and red flashes. This is a most pleasant track, shaded along its length by beech trees, and with good views.

4. After about 1.5km, the old railway track crosses a wide tarmacked road. Here the GR341 leaves you and turns left into the town. You continue ahead on the railway track, now marked with yellow flashes. The track passes under a road, and about 200 metres after this you should take a path leaving the railway and doubling back on the right. A yellow arrow on a tree directs you. In a further 200 metres, cross over a tarmacked road and continue ahead with woods on your right and views to the left.

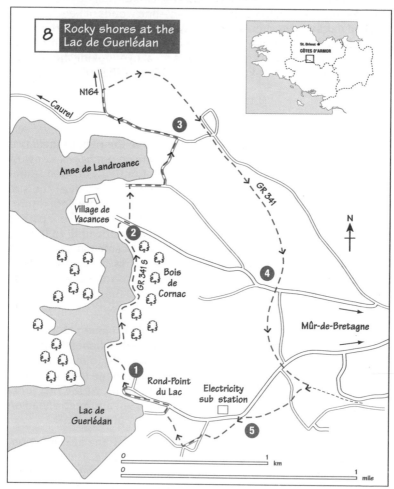

5. On reaching another tarmacked road opposite an electricity station, do not join it, but rather bear left on a waymarked track behind the hedge. This soon bears right and becomes a broad grassy track leading uphill. Where this reaches another metalled road, turn left uphill to reach a junction at a corner. Now turn right on a track beside a house (waymarked) and continue through the woods downhill. Cross over a track and continue downhill again. Almost immediately, bear left, again following the yellow flashes, on a wide track towards the lake. On reaching the road at the bottom, turn right and then left to return to the Rond-Point.

More Walks in the Area

The walk around the lake following the Grandes Randonnées all the way is about 48km – 30 miles! If this seems a little far, you could always take two days over it. This is quite a popular option, and there are several places to stay en route – Caurel, Bon Repos, Mûr-de-Bretagne and St Aignan all have accommodation.

If you are still thinking of rather shorter routes, the stylish new Office du Tourisme at Mûr-de-Bretagne has a lot to offer. Should you be staying for any length of time, you could make use of a pack of walking cards (*Balades et Petites Randonnées au Pays de Guerlédan et de Korong*), comprising about 20 walks and a few horse and bike rides, too. These cover the area to the north of the lake, which includes some spectacular gorges and megaliths as well as forest walks. A very

Beau Rivage at Caurel

pleasant route is the one entitled *Circuit des Landes* from Caurel (11km). Walking on the moors (landes) and through the woods above the lake, you reach the beach aptly named *Beau Rivage*. This is a fine spot for a swim and there are also restaurants offering resuscitation.

The countryside to the south of the lake is similarly pleasing. The leaflet *Randonnées St Aignan* (again obtainable from the Office du Tourisme in Mûr-de-Bretagne) has four walks ranging through forest to open countryside. All are colour-coded and very well waymarked – and easy to follow from the leaflet with no knowledge of French required. The orange circuit passes the barrage, the Chapel of Ste. Tréphine and the site of Castel-Finans (now with an orientation table), said to have once been the castle of the ferocious Baron Comorre.

Further afield, there are waymarked trails in the *Forêt de Quénécan,* a remaining part of the ancient forest of Argoat, in the south-west. There are also splendid walks in the rocky gorges to the north – Poulancre, Toul-Goulic and Daoulas (see Walk 9). For all these, the Office du Tourisme at Mûr-de-Bretagne – and that at Gouarec – should be able to give you details.

Places of interest nearby

The lakeside beach area of *Beau Rivage* at Caurel is just a few kilo-metres away – leaving the Rond-Point for Mûr-de-Bretagne, turn left where signed. Here there are camp-sites set in woodland above the water, a most attractive sandy beach, one or two interesting restau-rants, and rather modern glass-topped trip boats conducting frequent tours of the lake and even dinner cruises. In the French holiday months of July and August, all is in full swing – outside this time, you may well find things closed down, but the beach itself is attractive enough, and a good place for a swim if the weather is warm.

A different view of the barrage can be had from the car park above St Aignan. The huge concrete slope at the back is quite terrifying. If you would like to understand how water generates power, there are free tours here (1½ hours) – once more, only in July and August. From this car park, a short walk above the lake will bring you to the chapel of Ste. Tréphine and a fine viewpoint with an orientation table.

Back in St Aignan, there is a tiny electricity museum where it seems that bits of pylons and turbines are jumbled up with megaliths and picnic tables – a curious diversion, again only open in summer.

Dolmen de la Pierre Courcoulée, Forest of Fougères (walk 1)

'Les Roches Sculptés' – rock carving at Rothéneuf (walk 3)

Château de Trécesson (walk 6)

Beechwoods beside the canal at Hédé (walk 4)

Fencing of granite schist at Parsac (walk 5)

Woodland beside the Lac de Guerlédan (walk 8)

On the Customs Officers' Path, along the Pink Granite Coast (walk 10)

The harbour at Erquy, from the coastal path (walk 12)

9. Bon-Repos and the Gorges du Daoulas

At the heart of the Argoat, the River Daoulas cuts a dramatic gorge through the granite rock. This walk climbs from an old abbey beside the river to a high plateau above the gorge, where three remarkable ancient burial chambers conceal themselves amid the gorse and bracken.

Grade: Strenuous

Distance: 5.5km (3½ miles)

Time: 2 hours

Map: IGN Série Bleue 0818 0

Start and finish: Bon-Repos Abbey

How to get there: Bon-Repos Abbey is right in the centre of Brittany, just south of the N164 at the western end of the Lac de Guerlédan. Park where signed for the abbey – beside the road before it crosses the river.

Refreshment: There is a bar/crêperie beside the bridge over the Blavet, and a bar – the *Tavarn an Daoulas* – beside the main road. On the site of the abbey, the *Hôtellerie de l'Abbaye de Bon-Repos* is both hotel and restaurant in a beautiful setting. There is also a more informal *Café de l'Abbaye*. Should these be closed or otherwise inappropriate, there are all facilities in the little town of Guarec, 5km west.

Notes: The path up to the megaliths is steep – and the one down even steeper, and rocky as well. Add to this the ridge-top walk, and you can see that good footwear is needed. Walking boots are preferable. On a hot day it might be a good idea to take water – you will appreciate it after the climb. You might also like to bring binoculars as there are excellent views from the top

Waymarking: The track leading up to the megaliths is signed and waymarked in yellow, and thereafter you follow the white on red waymarking of GR to return to the road through the gorge.

Introduction

To the north of the Lac de Guerlédan is a high plateau of granite schist, a sort of eastern outpost of the Monts d'Arrée. These are some of the oldest hills in the world, formed in the primary era, about 600 million years ago. In this high plateau, the south flowing rivers cut deep gorges as they tumble to join the River Blavet below. Of these, the Gorges du Daoulas is quite spectacular, and you can follow it along a road that winds beside the river. But for those who travel on foot, there are even greater spectacles and this truly is a walk on the wild side – at least by Breton standards.

The walk starts gently enough at Bon-Repos Abbey, a 12th century Cistercian establishment beside the River Blavet. The descriptive name was inflicted by its founder, Alain, Vicomte de Rohan, an insomniac who finally achieved a good night's sleep here after a day spent hunting in the nearby forest. Wide grassy banks, picnic tables, a trip-boat and a restaurant complete the tranquil holiday scene. But leaving it, you are soon climbing quite steeply up the sides of the gorge – do not be deceived by that innocuous-looking granite sign pointing the way. Reaching the plateau at the top you are in the *lande*, the moorland. It is a landscape of gorse, broom, bracken and heather, quite wild, remote and very attractive. Hidden here, each in its own clearing, are the three *Allées Couvertes de Liscuis*, some of the best-preserved megaliths in the area. In summer, you may find one or two people who have survived the climb to reach them, but, out of season, the spot will almost certainly be deserted. It can be quite a mystical experience to walk beside these ancient tombs on a misty morning, alone on the roof of Brittany.

Allées Couvertes, or gallery graves, are the most elaborate of the megaliths – simpler are the *menhir*, a standing stone, and the *dolmen*, a stone table. An allée couverte is like a row of tables forming several chambers each having a purpose – one was an entrance hall, others were tombs and another contained objects needed in the after-life. The whole was then covered by an earthen mound or a cairn of stones. There are many such megaliths in this area and the explanation lies in the local discovery of a quarry of fine granite and a 'workshop' producing 'polished' axes, all dating from the Neolithic era, some 5000 to 2000 years BC. Axes from this quarry have been discovered all over France. To the north of the quarry was found an area of habitations, and to the south, an area of tombs. A granite display board beside your path points out the various features of these three allées couvertes.

Moving on from the megaliths, the path now becomes more demanding as you follow a Grande Randonnée beside the edge of the plateau. Here jagged teeth of quartz project along the rim of the gorge and – in the typical style of a Grande Randonnée – every crest is visited for you to appreciate the view. The ridge-top path and the subsequent descent into the gorge make this a walk not for the faint-hearted. But eventually the road is reached, and you return through the gorge beside the rushing river. Hopefully your exertions have induced a night of 'bon repos'.

The Walk

1. Walk up to join the main road and turn left along it (with care!). Immediately after crossing over the River Daoulas, a road on the right is signed to the Gorges du Daoulas. Ignore this and take the next road on the right a few metres further along. This road climbs and bends to the left. Ignore the first track off to the right just after the bend – even though it has Grande Randonnée waymarks – and continue for about 100 metres to another track where a granite sign points to the *Allées Couvertes* and is waymarked in yellow.

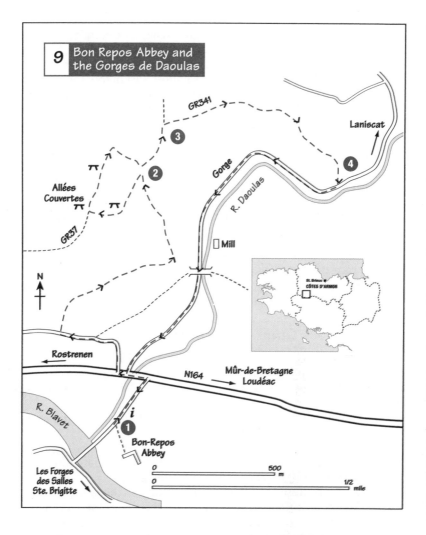

9 Bon Repos Abbey and the Gorges de Daoulas

The path first climbs gently through woodland where little sign-boards offer you the opportunity to learn the names of trees in French. After this, it climbs quite steeply, passing an old quarry and the site of a slate-workers hut. More climbing brings you to an information board telling you about the flora and fauna in the *lande* – you have a chance of seeing fox, badger, deer and even wild boar up here. The views are superb, and extend as you climb.

2. Reaching a cross-tracks at the summit, a granite sign on the left describes the features of the allées couvertes. Walking past it for 200 metres or so, you arrive at the first of these impressive megaliths. Its setting is equally impressive, with views for miles across

the coloured distant hills and wooded valleys. Continuing past the megalith, you reach another and turning sharp right here, a third. The track past this shortly brings you to a sort of T-junction where you turn right to reach a wooden signpost (just before the original track junction with the granite sign, Point 2). Now you turn left, following the direction of the GR341 towards Caurel. The GR is well-marked with the usual white and red bars and is easy to follow.

3. After about 300 metres, look out for a right fork – the path ahead is marked with a cross. Soon follows a fine ridge-walk, the path marked with both yellow and white on red waymarks that lead you on past various rocky outcrops with magnificent views. Eventually the path turns and makes a dramatic descent down the side of the gorge.

4. On reaching the road, turn right and follow it through the gorge and past the old water-mill – now ignoring all waymarking persuading you to turn left.. Continue instead to the main road, and here turn left and retrace your steps to the abbey.

Other Walks in the Area

The Office du Tourisme at Mûr-de-Bretagne stocks a very good pack of local walking cards, entitled *Balades et Petites Randonnées au Pays de Guerlédan et du Korong*. The following routes are just a selection from that pack

For another gorge walk, try the Gorges de Poulancre to the east, where the river of that name cuts a further deep forested wedge through the granite. From the pretty floral village of Saint-Gilles-Vieux-Marché, a waymarked route (8km, but rather less steep than this one) will take you through the gorge.

If you have acquired an interest in prehistory on this walk, another waymarked ramble (9km) takes you to visit the site of the aforementioned Neolithic axe-quarry at Quelfenec. The route starts from Plussulien, 12km to the north.

More recent historical remains can be found in the form of an old Roman aqueduct at Maël-Carhaix to the west. A short walk (4.5km) takes you along a sunken path deep in a valley, where the vestiges of the old aqueduct are pointed out on wayside signs.

A walk of contrasts is described on the card entitled *Les Landes de Liscuis*. Here the route starts from Bon-Repos Abbey and climbs to the allées couvertes again. It then follows the GR 37 along the plateau to the west. After about 5km, the path descends and crosses the N164 to join the towpath beside the River Blavet for a gentle walk home.

Although not mentioned in the pack of walks, the ancient Forêt de Quénécan to the south of Bon-Repos has many waymarked trails. Deer and wild boar are at home here and access to the forest is limited

Allée Couverte above the Gorges du Daoulas

in the months of *La Chasse* (the hunting and shooting season) – usually November to February. The Office du Tourisme at Mûr-de-Bretagne, Gouarec or Bon-Repos itself should be able to give you details of the paths – or just look at the display board over the river bridge by the abbey, and follow your chosen colour.

Places of interest nearby

Bon-Repos Abbey dates from the 12th century, was rebuilt in the 14th century and destroyed in the Revolution. Now there are only ruins, but along with them you can enjoy various craft workshops and exhibitions and even from time to time a *Son et Lumière*. A trip boat operates cruises along the canal from the river bridge

Les Salles des Forges (over the river bridge and follow the signs) is the site of an old iron and steel works opened by the Rohan family and dating from the 18th century. The scene is far from an industrial one – the preserved village with pool and gardens lies deep in the Forêt de Quénécan. Various buildings – the iron worker's house, chapel, school, etc. have been restored for visiting. Most impressive is the setting – beside the pool stand the ruins of the château that once belonged to the Rohans.

Just north of the Gorges is the village of Laniscat, known for its fine 16th /17th century church with a rare carillon of 25 bells, and the old quarry worker's house in blocks of granite schist. Further on is the chapel of Saint-Gildas with its three fountains – one for men, one for women and one to protect dogs from rabies! British dogs with their immunisations can give it a miss.

10. The Pink Granite Coast at Perros-Guirec

West of Perros-Guirec, the rocks of the Pink Granite coast take on the most bizarre of profiles, their rounded deep-coloured forms contrasting boldly with the azure sea. This walk follows the Sentier des Douaniers, the famous coastal path from Perros-Guirec to Ploumanac'h, and returns inland with many fine views.

Grade: Easy

Distance: 14km (8¾ miles) but the coastal section itself is 6km in length, and it is possible to make the return (or outward) journey by bus.

Time: 4 hours for whole route

Map: IGN TOP 25 0714 OT. Before you start, it is worth obtaining the booklet *Discovering the Footpaths along the Coast of Ploumanac'h*, which can be found in any local Office du Tourisme, and which is published in several languages, including English. Numbered blocks of pink granite mark the various sights along the Sentier des Douaniers, which are then described in the booklet.

Start and finish: Plage de Trestraou, Perros-Guirec

How to get there: Perros-Guirec is on the north coast, midway between St Brieuc and Morlaix. The Plage de Trestraou is the beach on the western side of the town. There is parking along the sea-front

Refreshment: There are many bars and restaurants at both the Plage de Trestraou and at Ploumanac'h. On the return route, there is more opportunity for resuscitation at La Clarté.

Notes: This is a walk on well-trodden paths and small roads – trainers would be quite adequate footwear. If you contemplate a diversion into the valley of the Traouïero (see below), you may appreciate walking boots in damp weather. There is little shade on much of this route. On a hot day, you should think of protection from the sun – and of carrying fluids, although it is possible to buy drink at Ploumanac'h and La Clarté. Swimming is possible along the route. The best beach is that of St Guirec at Ploumanac'h, although the tide goes out a long way. And if you want to look at off-shore islands – take your binoculars.

Waymarking: The coastal path is waymarked in white on red (a Grande Randonnée) – but you can't possibly get lost here. The latter part of the route is not waymarked.

Introduction

This has to be the most amazing of Brittany's coastal walks. The 'Pink Granite' rock is, in its natural state, a sort of dusky red colour and here the erosion of many millennia has rounded its corners, worked deep fissures and generally been the architect of the most eccentric of sea-scapes. This is a popular holiday area, and the path is well-known,

Plage de Trestraou, Perros-Guirec

so you are unlikely to have the scene to yourself. Nevertheless, this is a walk that should not be missed and you can always enjoy a little more solitude on the return route.

Leaving Perros-Guirec on the broad well-sign-posted track, you may, at first, wonder what all the fuss is about. The wide bay stretches before you, limited by a few humps of orange-glowing rock. Arriving at that rock, you are in a cove known as Pors Rolland – and the walk takes on another dimension. Beside the tiny cove, a weird convoluted pile of rocks called 'The Castle' shelters tall dark-green pines and you feel you have reached another world. From here the rock formations become more fantastic by the minute. Many have been given names – the foot, the chameleon, Napoleon's hat – but you can readily invent your own. The rocks of the Squewel tumble out on a peninsula into the sea and various others perform the most astonishing acts of balancing. The unworldly scenes continue, and reaching the cove of Pors Kamor, surrealism seems to have finally taken over. Here is a deep round pool of turquoise sea surrounded by grotesque shapes of darkest browny-red. Nearby is a lifeboat station, and, not far away, a lighthouse from which you can see the full length of this colourful coast. These shores are now a conservation area and the Maison du Littioral at Pors Kamor has a permanent exhibition.

St Guirec beach, although not without its rocks, seems something of a haven in this pageant. Behind the perfect horseshoe of its shores is the little town of Ploumanac'h where you can find welcome refreshment. Beside the beach is the chapel of St Guirec – he landed in this place in the 6th century, having crossed from Wales. Not far away, on rocks on the shore, stands the tiny oratory of St Guirec, a shelter containing a granite effigy of the saint. Legend has it that in addition to his healing skills he was adept at finding husbands. Any maiden who wishes to marry within the year has only to stick a pin in the nose of the saint – but even granite cannot withstand such onslaught, and the unfortunate St Guirec is now without a nose.

After the harbour at Ploumanac'h the route turns inland, passing above the valley of the Traouïero. Since Traouïero is Breton for 'Valleys', this seems to be the Valley of Valleys. And well it may be, since this is a most attractive place filled with dense woodland hiding more huge rocks of pink granite beside a tumbling river. A diversion into its depths is possible – but you may feel it merits more time on another day. The pink granite quarries themselves are passed as the route climbs to the village of la Clarté with its historic chapel. The final treat is the viewpoint with its orientation table at la Tertre, from where there is a fine panorama over the whole coast.

The Walk

1. From the western end of the Plage de Trestraou, a signpost to the *Sentier des Douaniers* directs you uphill on the road. As the road swings left, the coastal path leaves on the right. From this broad track there are now distant views of the pink granite outcrops ahead, and of the Sept Îles, the string of islands out to sea (there are actually only five of them!). Coming up to the first of the rocks, the path forks, and you bear to the right towards the coast. Soon you are in Pors Rolland, a most attractive cove guarded by a fissured rocky outcrop known as 'The Castle'

2. Pors Rolland marks the start of the curious rock formations. Following along the coast, you soon reach the Devil's Rock, falling abruptly into the sea. Odd rocks are poised precariously on others – The Bottle and The Sea-Tortoise – and the rocks projecting into the sea form the Squewel peninsula. A customs officers' lookout hut is passed and the tiny building hiding behind rocks was once a powder store for canons protecting the coast. Out to sea, on the Île aux Moines, you can just see the outlines of a Vauban fort. Soon you reach the cove of Pors Kamor. It is a place favoured by divers as the water at its entrance is something like 35 metres deep. Here is the lifeboat station and the Maison du Littoral. Beyond is the lighthouse, and after many more rocky exhibitions, the path turns inwards through an area of tropical vegetation to reach the beach of St Guirec.

3. As you reach the beach, the chapel and oratory of St Guirec are across the bay ahead. Follow the bay around, walk through the confines of the chapel and continue on the obvious path following the white on red bars of the Grande Randonnée. The path climbs up through some rocks and then descends with some good views of the château on the Île de Costaérès. A Polish architect designed

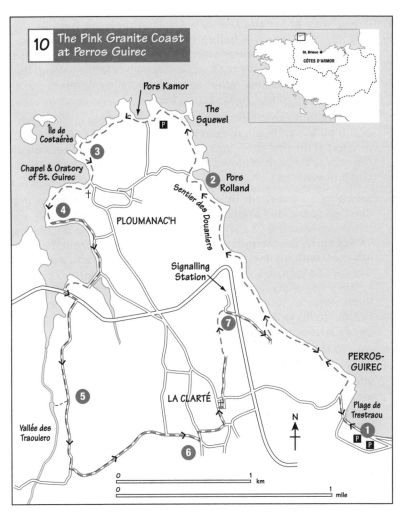

this château and it was lived in for a time by Henryk Sienkiewicz, who completed the writing of his novel *Quo Vadis* in this strange place. The path continues to the harbour at Ploumanac'h

4. Follow the road around the harbour to the far side, and then leave it to cross the estuary on the dam. The building at its end is a tide-mill. Continue following the waymarks around the edge of the estuary to reach the road beside the bridge. Now leave the GR and turn left along the road. Take the first road on the right (approx. 100 metres), signposted to the Site des Traouïero. This road climbs and passes through a village. After about 500 metres, on the right, you reach a sign board telling you of the paths in the Valley of the Traouïero.

5. If you wish to sample the valley, follow the path here to the bottom, cross the river before the lake, and keeping left, cross back on the second bridge after the lake. Keeping uphill on this path, you will rejoin the road some 400 metres farther along. But you may feel that this rather spectacular valley deserves more time – see the More Walks section below.

    The main route continues along the road with views (and sounds) of the pink granite quarries to the left. After about 500 metres, turn left at the first road junction and descend in the direction of the quarries. The road passes the entrance gates, and continues to climb towards La Clarté.

6. Reaching a cross-roads in the village, cross straight over on the Rue de Triagoz, and at its end, turn left. Next, bear right and then left to arrive at the Chapelle de la Clarté. The story is that in the 14th century, the Marquis de Barac'h was returning from the English coast with his fleet. A thick mist engulfed them and wind and tide carried them to rocks they could not see. The Marquis prayed to the Virgin Mary, and promised her a chapel if she would save them. A ray of sunshine broke through showing them the land. Faithful to his word, the Marquis built the chapel of Notre Dame de la Clarté at the place illuminated by that shaft of light.

    Pass behind the chapel (keeping the chapel on your left), and coming to a road, cross straight over on to the Rue du Tertre. Soon you arrive at the viewpoint and orientation table in a wide grassy area on the left. There are fine views over the Sept Îles and the coast, as well as much more inland. Keep ahead on the track, ignoring tracks on the left and finally reach a narrow tarmacked road, which swings right to come down to the main road.

7. Cross the main road and take a road approx. 30 metres down on the right, the Rue des Fougères. This descends quite steeply, and soon you reach a track junction, where you double back to the left to descend still farther to reach the coastal path again. Turn right and retrace your steps to Perros-Guirec.

More Walks in the Area

The GR 34 follows all the north coast of Brittany (the west and south, too). But if you want some more spectacles in pink granite, follow it west just 5km more to Trégastel. Again, this is on a bus route from Ploumanac'h and Perros-Guirec. A further 20km (a day's walk) brings you to Trébeurden – and the bus connections are still available. Ask at the Office du Tourisme in Perros-Guirec for details. It is always easy to follow a Grande Randonnée as they are so well waymarked, but you might like to see the route on the TOP 25 map mentioned above.

The valley of the Traouïero is quite spectacular, with huge granite boulders in precarious positions beside – and above – your path.

Caves in the rocks, viewpoints and rare vegetation make an interesting walk. The path follows the river to Kerrougant, a distance of about 3km, with various side-tracks. The routes are shown on boards at the entrances to the valley and in a leaflet *Vallée des Traouïero*, obtainable from Tourist Information.

Just west of Trégastel, the Île Grande is connected by causeway to the mainland. The coastal path circling the island is 7km in length. and is marked with the white on red flashes of a Grande Randonnée. There is lots of interest – coastal scenery, viewpoints, good beaches, an ornithological centre, an allée couverte (gallery grave) and a pine-clad island where it is said King Arthur (of Round Table fame) is buried. The route is easy to follow but it is described – in French – in a leaflet entitled *Pleumeur-Bodou, Île Grande*. This is one of a series of about 20 routes produced by the local communities along the Pink Granite coast – any Office du Tourisme should stock the collection.

The above mentioned series also contains leaflets describing the walks of the Pink Granite coast. But if you feel you have had enough of the coast, prehistoric megaliths are well-represented with circuits at Pleumeur-Bodou and Trébeurden. The latter route of 8km visits several menhirs (one in the sea) and an allée couverte.

Places of interest nearby

This walk passes the Maison du Littoral at Pors Kamor. You can also reach it by road from Ploumanac'h if you would prefer to return later. There are display boards on the formation of granite, a presentation on its uses and a photographic exhibition of the curious rock formations. The Maison is open from mid-June to mid-September only.

The gleaming white sphere of the Radôme at Pleumeur-Bodou can be seen from the viewpoint at la Tertre. It makes an exciting visit. This is the headquarters of French telecommunications research – its finest hour was in 1962, when it received the first satellite transmission from across the Atlantic via Telstar. The Musée des Telecommunications is situated beside the dome – with many hands-on exhibits, it tells the story of message sending from Morse Code to the complexities of the present day. The Radôme itself puts on the 'very latest technology show', a sort of sci-fi Son-et-Lumière, of which there is a daily English version. Beside the Radôme is the Planetarium de Bretagne, which also puts on an English performance – 'A voyage through the Solar System'

The Sept Îles provide one of the most interesting bird sanctuaries off the coast of Brittany. Many rare species – including puffins – breed here, but leave the islands in late summer. Boat trips depárt from both Perros-Guirec and Ploumanac'h in season and circle the islands, but landing is permitted only on the Île aux Moines (where you can visit the lighthouse and the Vauban fort). Take your binoculars – there is lots to see, possibly including a colony of grey seals.

11. Woods above the estuary of the Trieux

The River Trieux has cut deeply into the granite schist in the last stages of its journey to the sea. This is a walk along the wooded slopes high above the estuary, with magnificent views all the way. And if the distance is a little too great for you – you can always return by train.

Grade: Moderate

Distance: 12km (7½ miles)

Time: 4 hours

Map: IGN Top 25 0814 OT. A free leaflet (*Forêt Littorale entre Mer et Rivière*) including a map of the routes is available from the Mairie at Plourivo and from the Maison d'Estuaire on the walk.

Start and finish: Site de Frinaudour, near Plourivo

How to get there: From Paimpol, take the D15 south-west to Plourivo, and continue on the D82 through Penhoat to reach the estuary. There is a small parking area at the end of the road.

Refreshment: None. Take your picnic with you.

Notes: This walk is mostly on good tracks, which would be suitable for trainers in dry summer weather. At other times, wear your walking boots. Most of the walk is through woodland, offering pleasant shade on a hot day. The route does involve some climbing and descending, although nothing too strenuous. Don't forget to take food and lots of fluid. The return is across attractive moorland – but you can choose instead to catch the train from the halt at Lancerf. You can find the times at the stations (Frinaudour, Maison de l'Estuaire, Lancerf) or from the Office du Tourisme at Paimpol. All these stations are request stops – you just flag down the train. It does work – but if your walk would be spoiled by doubts, you can do things back-to-front and first catch the train from Lancerf.

Waymarking: The paths are mostly well-waymarked – in yellow and orange, with the occasional signpost. Occasionally, the plot seems to be lost – but it seems the marking is being renewed, and the free map is very good.

Introduction

The official guide to the Cotes d'Armor declares "It's a shame that there is no road along the Trieux estuary". Far from it! Here in the heart of holiday Brittany is a place where the mighty automobile cannot venture, where the splendid views of the estuary and the fine woodland are for walkers alone – or almost alone, since the other way to enjoy them is to take the train.

This area certainly is popular with holidaymakers. Not far away is the Point de l'Arcouest and the Île de Bréhat, the port of Paimpol and

Site de Frinaudour

some fine sandy beaches along a most attractive stretch of coast. But the Bois de Penhoat-Lancerf, sweeping down to the estuary of the Trieux, are definitely 'off the beaten track' and are well worth discovering. Despite their absence from the guidebooks, these woods are well-managed, with excellent paths and good waymarking – and a regular train service. The views are quite splendid and there is lots of interest along the way.

The walk starts from the Site de Frinaudour, beside the confluence of the Leff and the Trieux. The place is very peaceful and picturesque, the silence broken only by the occasional train crossing the Leff viaduct. The slight widening at the end of the road is hardly a car park – and, as the river here is tidal, take good care where you park your car if the water is low. From Frinaudour the path climbs quite steeply and is soon high above the river with some fine views. Almost opposite, the imposing Château of Roche-Jagu looks down from a similar height. Built in the 15th century to command the river, its interior is surprisingly Renaissance – and its exceptional 'modern' medieval gardens attract many visitors. The path descends through woods of chestnut and oak to the site of Coat-Ermit, on the inside of the river bend opposite the château. Here you come across some old 'retting' tanks – tanks once used for soaking flax to remove the green parts and leave the fibres to make linen. The process produced such a powerful all-pervading smell that the tanks had to be located in a place as remote as possible from human habitation. A board (in French and English) explains the whole process.

Beyond Coat-Ermit, the next riverside site is that of the Manoir de Traou Nez – now become the Maison de l'Estuaire, owned by the *Conservatoire du Littoral* and dedicated to the protection of these woods and riverside. The old stone house stands in a clearing in the trees just above the river. As the Manoir de Traou Nez, the house was, in 1923, the scene of a famous murder which has remained unsolved – a case referred to rather enigmatically as the Seznec affair. The somewhat spooky setting here seems one Agatha Christie might have aspired to. After more climbing, cliffs and woodland, you have a choice – return over the moorland above the estuary or continue to the village of Lancerf and catch the train. If you choose the latter, you can see some 13th century crosses near the roadside and visit the tiny rustic chapel at Lancerf where a son of Napoleon is buried. The moorland route offers easy walking on springy-turfed paths lined by gorse, pines and heather – a pleasant return to the riverside at Frinaudour.

The Walk

1. From the estuary at Frinaudour, walk back up the road, pass under the viaduct, and take the first road on the left, which goes steeply uphill. Pass the railway halt on your left, and farther on, take the track on the left, just after the first house. A marker post directs you to Coat-Ermit. This narrow track bears right and climbs through the trees to reach a broad track at a T-junction. Turn left here, still following signs to Coat Ermit. Now suddenly there are fine views across the estuary – you are almost opposite the castle of Roche-Jagu. The path goes on across gorse and heather and through woodland of chestnut and beech. At one point, you divert to skirt behind a house, after which the track narrows a little but is still obvious. Eventually you descend to the road at Coat Ermit.

2. The road to your left descends to reach the banks of the river on a sharp bend – a distance of about 500 metres. Your path continues ahead, and is now signed to Traou Nez. On the left, where the path leaves the road, are the old retting tanks for the flax. Continuing ahead through the woodland, you soon reach a sort of path cross-roads, where you cross straight over. Orange and yellow bands a few metres on down the track confirm you are on the right road. The path again runs through woodland high above the river, and as you pass under the high-tension lines, you have another fine view of Roche-Jagu. Descending now to a valley, you come close to the railway line and a path junction. It seems that you can go to Traou Nez via the yellow route to the right or the orange route to the left. Take the latter, which descends to cross the stream at the bottom of the valley. The path then joins the stream to pass through a tunnel under the railway. Continuing ahead on the far side, the waymarks have become yellow again.

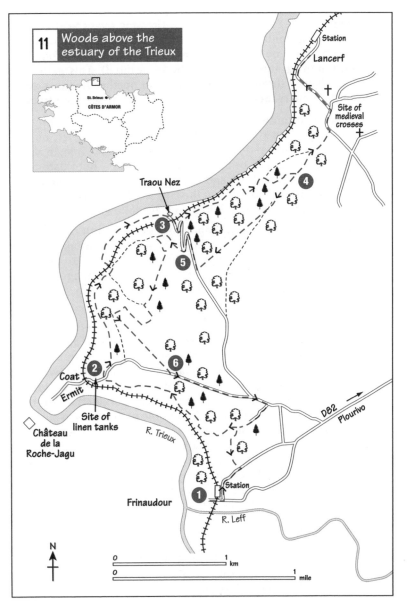

11 Woods above the estuary of the Trieux

St. Brieuc
CÔTES D'ARMOR

Station

Lancerf

Site of medieval crosses

Traou Nez

3

4

5

2

Coat
Ermit

Site of linen tanks

6

D82 → Plourivo

R. Trieux

Château de la Roche-Jagu

1

Station

Frinaudour

R. Leff

N

0 — 1 km
0 — 1 mile

The path goes down to the edge of the river, and follows it to reach the Maison de l'Estuaire at Traou Nez.

3. Now follow the road under the railway, climbing uphill away from the river. At the hairpin bend to the right, take the track on the left, signposted to Lancerf. Again this is magnificent woodland with a preponderance of chestnuts – and, of course, pines. The path reaches a valley and curves inland. Crossing over the stream, it bears left and continues climbing with good views to reach a track junction. Here you bear left (there is a signpost but its wording has been removed – perhaps it will be re-instated). This path now wends its way through young pines and heather heading away from the estuary. Soon it arrives at a wide hard-surfaced track.

4. If you wish to continue to the station at Lancerf, turn left here and keep straight ahead to descend to the road. Turning left on this brings you to Lancerf (turning right on the road, and then, in about 100 metres, left, will bring you to the crosses – both date from around the 13th century, and are thought to be associated with battles against the Normans or the English). Heading again for the station in Lancerf, keep left in the village following the signs..

    To complete the circuit to Frinaudour on foot, turn right on the broad track and keep to it for about 350 metres. Now take a grassy track that leaves on the right, at an angle of about 20° to the main track. In about 800 metres this grassy track arrives at a road – this is actually the road running down to Traou Nez again. Turn right and keep to the road around two hairpin bends

5. Just after the second bend, take the track on the left. This track climbs uphill into the woods again, and, after about 300 metres, reaches a track junction. The broader path ahead goes downhill slightly, but you turn sharp left and climb on a track winding through the pines. Waymarks appear as you go, and you follow them across the top of the hill. At the junction under the high-tension lines, you go straight ahead. After the path begins to curve to the right, another junction is reached, and you cross the stream to go straight ahead in the direction of Coat Ermit. The path continues to curve around, but soon you reach another junction, in a clearing. Here take the broad grassy track on the left with banks of pine trees set back on either side. Keeping straight ahead on this will bring you to the road – the road to Coat Ermit.

6. Turn left on this road. In about 700 metres, keep ahead (right) at the road junction. After a further 100 metres or so, take the first road on the right, the Route de Ker Bruc. A waymarking post stands in the hedge opposite. Descending on this road, in about 300 metres you reach a track on the left – the track you came up earlier at the outset of the walk. The marker post indicates only Coat-Ermit (straight ahead), but on the other side you will see Frinaudour signed. Turn left down this track and, finally turning right on the road, retrace your steps to the riverside.

More Walks in the Area

All the footpaths, cycle routes and horse trails in this area are shown on the leaflet *Forêt Littorale entre Mer et Rivière* (see **Map** section above). Another interesting route shown on this leaflet follows the south bank of the River Leff from the confluence at Frinaudour. The path is well-waymarked (it is actually a Grande Randonnée), and goes on to cross the river at the Pont de Houel. Continuing beside the water, it arrives at the Moulin de Guézennec, a mill recently restored. Unfortunately, the return would have to be along the same route, since there is no other river bridge. It is also possible to follow the same Grande Randonnée (the GR 341) from Frinaudour upstream along the banks of the Trieux.

The other Grande Randonnée in the area, the famous coastal path, the GR 34, arrives on the east bank of the Trieux having crossed the bridge from Lézardrieux. It then follows the Trieux to the sea and arrives at the delightful port of Loquivy – apparently a favourite haunt of Lenin! Continuing, it skirts the coast to the Point de l'Arcouest – a spectacular journey with wonderful sea views across to the Île de Bréhat. The route then heads south to Paimpol, once the home of an Icelandic fishing fleet. On the way it passes the widows cross at Pors-Even, where the wives of missing fishermen looked hopefully out to sea, and the little chapel at Perros-Hamon where the names of lost fishermen are written in the church porch. The route of the GR is shown on the IGN map named above – and, of course, the waymarking is first-rate. There is a bus service between Paimpol and the Pointe de l'Arcouest, which makes this part of the route easily accessible, but if you want to extend your range, think of taking a taxi. The Office du Tourisme in Paimpol will help you with arrangements.

If you would like to walk this coast, but would prefer circular routes, the Office du Tourisme at Paimpol should be able to find you a leaflet entitled *Ploubazlanec – Randonnées Pédestres*. Six waymarked circuits are shown on a clear map.

The Île de Bréhat itself makes interesting walking. It is in fact two islands, united by a bridge built by Vauban in the 18th century. There are many footpaths on the island, but the whole circuit is about 15km with lots to see – chapel, tide-mill, harbours, woods, lighthouses, and pink shingle beaches.

And if you are spending all your holiday in this area, think of getting the Topoguide *Entre Manche et Guerlédan (Ref. 070)* – you should find it in most bookshops and even in supermarkets. There are many waymarked circuits on the coast from l'Arcouest in the north to St Brieuc in the south. This, like most Topoguides, is published only in French, but you should have little trouble following the routes from maps and waymarking alone if necessary.

Places of interest nearby

The Château de la Roche-Jagu is a fine edifice dating from medieval times – but the most impressive feature is its gardens. The grounds actually cover about 30 hectares and there are three waymarked walks. Besides these, there are walled gardens, water gardens, camellia woods, foreign gardens and a lot more. The park is open free of charge throughout the year, but the house, which puts on exhibitions, is open only in the summer months, with a modest entrance fee.

It is well worth taking the crossing to the Île de Bréhat, just 15 minutes from the Point de l'Arcouest. On this idyllic island, no cars are allowed (although tractors are), and you can enjoy the lush Mediterranean vegetation of mimosas and figs and hydrangeas and admire the elegant holiday homes of affluent Parisians. Sea views are superb in every direction – and for the very best, you can climb a Buchan-esque 39 steps to the viewpoint at La Chapelle St Michel, from where you look out over a myriad of islands. For more solitude – head north and cross the bridge to the north island. It may be a little more barren, but the crowds thin as you go.

Just a few kilometres south of Paimpol is the Abbaye de Beauport, an abbey dating from the 13th century, in a splendid setting beside the sea. This was once a stopping place on the pilgrimage route to Santiago da Compostela. Now the graceful ruins are being restored and you can view the church, cloisters, chapter house, refectory and plenty more, all in picturesque surroundings. The abbey is open all year, but a series of evening concerts is an added summer attraction.

12. Cliffs and coves around the Cap d'Erquy

The north coastal path of Brittany, the GR34, must be one of the most scenic footpaths in Europe. Here it is at its very best, giving you a magnificent walk along the clifftops, with fine views of the rocky coast and the fishing harbour at Erquy.

Grade: Moderate (with difficult option towards the end)

Distance: 9.5km (6 miles)

Time: 2½ hours

Map: IGN Top 25 0916 ET

Start and finish: The port at Erquy

How to get there: Erquy is on the north coast, about 20km north of Lamballe. The port is at the north end of the town beach. There is parking all along the promenade and in various other sites in the town. It is also possible to start this walk from the car park at the Plage du Guen (Point 2) or the car park on the Cap d'Erquy (just after Point 3)

Refreshment: There are many bars and restaurants along the sea-front at Erquy – everything from an ice-cream to a five-course meal is readily available.

Notes: This is an easy walk suitable for trainers. Near the end, there is a rather adventurous option around the cliffs, which you should not even consider if you have children with you. It does, however, have its rewards. Take swimming costumes (Erquy has safe beaches) – and binoculars for the distant sea views. On a hot day, you might like to carry fluids – and don't forget the sun cream.

Waymarking: Most of the walk follows the GR34 and so has white on red waymarks. The town section is not waymarked.

Introduction

The fishing port of Erquy is famed for its scallops – *Coquilles Saint-Jacques*. You can see them in crates beside the harbour and you can eat them in the many restaurants along the sea front. With a fleet of more than 80 boats, this is a fishing port in the most picturesque of settings – tucked beneath high cliffs and looking out on a perfect horse-shoe bay fringed by pines. It is, of course, popular with holiday makers, and July and August can see the town quite crowded. But there is plenty of space for everyone on the seven beaches of white sand, of which Erquy is justly proud.

Above Erquy is a plateau of land that for the last thirty years has been designated an area of outstanding natural beauty. This is the Cap d'Erquy, a land where heather, gorse, bracken and pine trees, turquoise sea and white-edged rocks stun you with their perfect combi-

Boats on the quay at Erquy

nation. And there are distant views – behind you, Cap Fréhel with its lighthouse, and ahead, the wide sweep of the Bay of St Brieuc leading to the Point de l'Arcouest and the Île de Bréhat.

The walk here starts from the port and crosses the promontory to reach the coast and the GR34 at the Plage du Guen, one of those fine sandy beaches. Climbing then to the cliffs and the cape, this is a walk with a truly splendid setting, which has lots more of interest before you return. Continuing from the cape, the route passes a little grey stone building that was once a unit in the scheme of coastal defences set up by Louis XVI in the 18th century. Close by and looking out to sea is another little grey stone building with much more sinister connections. Called a *Four à Boulets*, it was built around 1794 as a kiln to raise cannon-balls to 'red heat' before firing, in order to set fire to wooden ships. Its primary target was the English fleet! From here, the descent into Erquy on the Grande Randonnée is something of an experience as the path clings to the cliff-face – and it is an experience you may choose to do without. But taking the cliff path will provide you with a unique bird's eye view of the fishing fleet and harbour. It will also take you past Les Lacs Bleus (although they look brown), which were apparently left after quarrying stone here to build the pavements of Paris in the 19th century. A return along the road is a safer alternative, but whatever you choose, Erquy is waiting at the bottom of the hill and you should not miss the Coquilles Saint-Jacques!

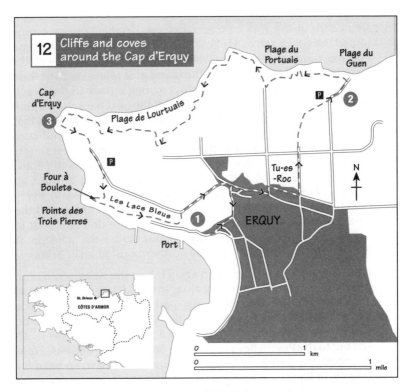

The Walk

1. Leave the promenade at the northern end, at the corner with the paved triangle, where the road bears left towards the harbour. At this corner is an alley, the Chemin des Coches, marked with the white on red flashes of the Grande Randonnée. These lead you up some steps to emerge on a wide road. Turn left and shortly, bear left off the road following the Grande Randonnée waymarks through some houses and up a steep flight of steps to join another road. Here turn right past the Erquy sign (the GR goes left here) and at the road junction, turn left uphill on the Rue des Grès Rose. You are now on the edge of Tu es Roc with its lovely old houses and have glimpses of sea views on the right-hand side. Turn left on the Rue de Pâques (S.P. le Portuais), and then take the first right – Rue de Tennis. After passing the tennis courts on the left, turn left down the Rue de Portuais. Continue ahead (a road crosses) to the barrier at the bottom. On the far side of the barrier, take the right-hand track leading slightly uphill through the pines to reach the car park at Plage de Guen.

2. From the car park, walk through the barriers, heading downhill. At the second small parking area on the left, take the track up the

steps and, at the fork of the tracks, bear right. You have now joined the GR34 and can follow its waymarks. As you climb to the cliff-top there are fine views behind you – Cap Fréhel with its lighthouse, and, much nearer, the island of St Michel with its little chapel on top. Again you descend, crossing a track to the beach (now the Plage de Portuais), and then, at the next track, turn uphill on a rather daunting flight of over 100 steps. The good news is that you are spared the last 5 or so – here you turn right on a well-concealed, but again waymarked track. This stretch of coast is simply beautiful. The way continues, down valleys and across cliff-tops, well-waymarked at every junction, to reach the tip of the Cap d'Erquy. From this wild promontory, there are views in every direction. Close at hand you can see the town of Erquy and the lovely beaches all the way along to the Pointe de Pléneuf at le Val-André. Beyond the land swings out across the Baie de St Brieuc to the Île de Bréhat and the northernmost point of Brittany.

3. From the Cap you turn left, and again follow the waymarked path to reach a car park. Continuing along the road, you can see ahead the little grey building that was part of the coastal defence scheme. Just before reaching it, the waymarks of the Grande Randonnée lead you to turn right on a tiny path. This now leads you out to the Pointe des Trois Pierres and its *Four à Boulets*. From this point, the path becomes precarious – if you have no head for heights, or have children with you, you may prefer to return to the road and continue that way. The path rejoins the road in about 800 metres.

If you have decided to stick with the path, you will find it well-waymarked. At times it is seemingly cut from the cliffside and at one point there is an excellent view of the harbour – you are suspended vertically above it. The path also passes the 'blue' lakes left after quarrying and eventually emerges on the road. Here you turn right and, skirting behind the château, descend towards the town. Just before the ERQUY sign, you will reach the top of the steps you came up earlier, and can retrace your steps following the GR waymarks to reach the port and sea-front

More Walks in the Area

The GR34 continues along the coast to both east and west and there are bus services in both directions – ask at the Office du Tourisme. They could also help you out with a taxi if you would find it easier.

Heading westwards, it is just 10km by the coastal path to the pleasant resort of Pléneuf-Val-André. The path runs beside and above several excellent beaches backed by pine woods. After Pléneuf, which itself has a magnificent sandy beach, the path continues, and in another 4km reaches the most attractive fishing port of Dahouët.

Walking in an easterly direction, 13km on the GR34 will bring you to the resort of Sables-d'Or-les-Pins. The route passes the little island of St Michel with its chapel, which can be reached on foot at low tide, and continues across the very attractive estuary of the River Islet. Sables-d'Or–les-Pins has an interesting history – see Places of Interest, below.

If you can continue past Sables-d'Or-les-Pins, it is a further 15km to Cap Fréhel. This windswept and rocky promontory, 70 metres above the emerald sea, is a fine view point – and you can climb the lighthouse to extend your range. Beware the crowds in summer, but out of season you may even have this elemental place to yourself. Long and short circular walking routes around Cap Fréhel are described in various leaflets, and you can also visit Fort la Latte, 4km farther around the coast. This well-preserved fort was again part of the coastal defence. Check at the Office du Tourisme in Erquy for walking routes and details of Fort la Latte.

The Office du Tourisme has itself produced a collection of short circular walks near Erquy, accompanied by photocopied maps. Most of these routes are not waymarked, but it should be possible to follow them from the map alone if the French text proves too much. The complete circuit of the cape, returning on a disused railway track makes an excellent – if rather long (20km) – tour of the area. If you are feeling energetic, you could consider it as an alternative to the walk described.

Places of interest nearby

Pléneuf-Val-André, 10km west, has one of the finest beaches on the north coast of Brittany. From the Pointe de Pléneuf there are more excellent coastal views, and the GR34 itself continues south of the town as the very pleasant Chemin de la Guette, leading to the charming fishing port of Dahouët. Just off Pléneuf is the Île de Verdelet – an island bird sanctuary, which can be reached on foot at the lowest of tides.

Les Sables-d'Or-les-Pins is a purpose-built resort – or, it should have been. The golden sand was imported and the fine residences behind were built at the end of the 19th century to attract the wealthy from the cities. Unfortunately war intervened, much money was lost and it was never completed. Nevertheless, it now offers a most attractive beach fringed by pines and is popular for water-sports.

And if you want to get right away from all beaches, try the Château de Bien-Assis, inland, between Erquy and Pléneuf. It was built of pink Erquy sandstone around the 16th century and you can visit an assortment of rooms and the French gardens.

13. In the valley of the River Arguenon

The deep wooded valley of the River Arguenon is a sharp contrast to the otherwise gently rolling countryside of this part of Brittany. This fairly energetic walk through that valley starts from the splendid Château de la Hunaudaye, a castle with medieval inhabitants.

Grade: Moderate to strenuous

Distance: 9.5km (6 miles)

Time: 2½ hours

Map: IGN Top 25 1016 ET

Start and finish: Château de la Hunaudaye

How to get there: The Château de la Hunaudaye is near the village of Plévin, 16km east of Lamballe. From Plévin, take the D28 in the direction of St Aubin, and turn where signed to the Château. There is a car park beside the road just past the Château.

Refreshment: The lovely farm beside the Château boasts a Crêperie, open every day in July and August and at weekends only in May, June and September. Near the start of the walk you pass the Auberge de Bélouze, a 16th century manor-cum-farm-cum-hostelry. This Auberge claims to serve everything from simple meals to medieval banquets, perhaps to complement the Château. If you prefer to do it yourself, there are picnic tables beside the viewpoint at Tournemine.

Notes: The path through the woodland can be muddy in winter or after summer rain, making boots preferable at such times. There are also one or two steep sections, which could be slippery. It is an ideal walk for a hot day as most of the route is in deep shade – but you might like to carry fluid with you as there is no refreshment en route.

Waymarking: The route is waymarked throughout in yellow or yellow on red.

Introduction

The five-towered Château de la Hunaudaye has something of a chequered history. Built around 1200, it was destroyed, rebuilt two centuries later, enlarged, burned down by the Republicans in the Revolution and left in ruins. The French government rescued it in 1930 and since then it has been at least partially restored. Now it is quite an imposing sight, complete with moat, drawbridge and towers, standing at the edge of its eponymous forest. In summer, flags fly outside and folk in medieval attire can be seen flitting about the grassy banks as they act out everyday life in the 14th century. Out of season, the audience is often school children, but July and August bring in the tourists. Whether or not you venture inside, the setting itself is quite photogenic – and just up the road is an excellent crêperie in a lovely old stone farmhouse, just right for the end of the walk.

From the Château the route leads you through pleasant country-

Château de la Hunaudaye

side to the banks of the River Arguenon. Here the river has been dammed to provide a water supply and there is now a twisting ribbon lake some ten miles long in a surprisingly deep valley. The forest spills over the steep slopes to the water's edge and creates an attractive scene where, under a canopy of green, wild flowers thrive in the dappled light. The winding path climbs and descends through the woodland, offering views from rocky heights soon followed by close encounters with the reedy shores. At times the path is flanked by dense vegetation and long fronds of climbing plants hang from the trees. You could be forgiven for thinking you were in the African jungle – at least on a hot day. The path continues all the way around the lake – a distance of 35km or so. If you are feeling dynamic, you could choose to complete the circuit. But the walk here climbs out of the valley, beside a bubbling stream, and soon returns you to the Château – and its crêperie – both worthy of attention.

The Walk

1. From the car park, walk down the road passing the Château on the left. At the fork, keep right, heading towards St Jean, and take the first stony track on the right, which is waymarked in yellow and red. This track climbs gently uphill and soon there are distant views. On reaching the road, cross straight over (although the waymarking directs you left here) towards Bélouze. After descending the hill, the road forks, and again you head right, in the direction of Bélouze, picking up once more the yellow on red

waymarks, Still going downhill, the old Auberge is now on your right. In addition to the tempting restaurant, you can sample the garden of aromatic plants. At the bottom of the hill, the road bears left, and you continue along it to the cross-roads, just before la Fougeray. Here you turn left towards Tournemine, and the road now descends to a parking place and picnic spot beside a view-point on the lake.

2. Just before the road bridge, turn left on to the track beside the water, and then immediately, left uphill on a grassy track. Turning right at the top of this, you are on a path which, from this point, is waymarked either in yellow or yellow on red. Shortly the track descends, and there is a surprise right-hand turn going sharply downhill, waymarked on a tree. Look out for it! The route then takes you over a stream on a plank bridge and climbs again on the other side. The roller-coaster path continues, until after a big descent and another stream-crossing, a broad track is reached where you should turn right. At the next junction, bear right down beside the water and then bend away from the water following the path uphill and crossing another plank bridge. Continue up the very steep broad track heading away from the river, ignoring the little track along the water's edge. There are no waymarks here. On meeting the track coming in on the left, keep straight ahead, where you will soon be pleased to see again a waymarked tele-graph pole.

3. At the junction with the metalled road, cross straight over (yellow arrow painted on the road) and go straight ahead to where the hard-surfaced road becomes a grassy track. Continuing ahead in the woodland, there are fine views up an inlet to the east. After a descent, there is a sharp zig-zag climb to reach a grassy track again. Now bearing right on another grassy track (again waymarked), you will find yourself high above the river. The path continues past a danger sign on a steep descent – a sign presum-ably for cyclists (we are now on a VTT route) who, if missing the sharp left turn at the bottom, could go straight over the cliff-side! Walkers fortunately have more time to put on the brakes. Once down at the water's edge, the way follows it around and up the reedy creek to the west. Here keep to the waymarked lower track. Soon the head of the creek is passed and you continue over entrant streams to follow beside the main stream of this dense valley. A signpost directs you to the left to the Château de la Hunaudaye (the times are for cyclists!) and you continue climbing beside the stream.

4. On reaching the tarmacked road, turn right through the attractive hamlet of St Jean, and follow the road ahead, past the junction, to reach the Château de la Hunaudaye.

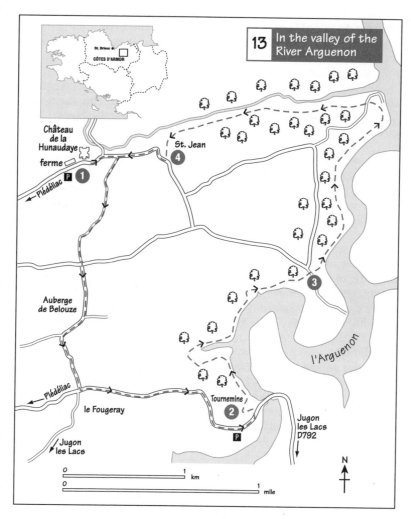

More Walks in the Area

There is a footpath all around this lake from Jugon-les-Lacs in the south to the bridge at Plévin in the north – a distance of about 35km On this sort of track, the whole journey would take something like 10 hours. But fortunately the circuit can be divided into three loops by the bridges at Tournemine and at Lorgeril – the top loop is then 17km, the middle just 8km, and the southern one, 10.5km – and you can walk the whole route in two or three days. If you prefer routes that also include some of the local countryside as well, there are several waymarked circuits on either side of the lake. The Office du Tourisme at Jugon-les-Lacs has details. You can also find these walks (and about 80 more) in the Topoguide *De la Côte d'Émeraude au Mené (Ref 037)* which is on sale at Tourist Offices, bookshops and even supermarkets! The French text can seem fairly daunting, but if you have tried this walk, you will know that good waymarking in addition to the maps will help you get around.

For yet more lakeside walks, Jugon-les-Lacs has its own lake to the south of the town. The circuit of this lake is about 16km but the terrain here is more open and the route passes through several villages. Other circuits including just part of the lake are also possible – once again, enquire at the Office du Tourisme.

If you would like your forest without the lake, there are waymarked paths and circuits in the Forêt de la Hunaudaye. This is rather a dense dark forest, and can be quite muddy in winter. It is closed for *la chasse* from mid-September to the end of February on Mondays, Thursdays and Saturdays.

Places of interest nearby

The Château de la Hunaudaye itself invites you to discover 'the everyday life of a 14th century Breton castle'. The company of actors Compagnie Mac'htiern are to be seen playing their medieval roles every day except Saturday in July and August, and on Sundays and bank holidays in May, June and September. Guided visits are also possible at other times. Any nearby Office du Tourisme can confirm times and details

At the village of Saint-Esprit-des-Bois, 2km west of Tournemine, an eco-museum known as La Ferme d'Antan is well worth a visit. This faithfully reconstructs the daily life of a farm at the beginning of the 20th century – with plenty of animals, tools of the time, countryside crafts, a forge and even crops now rarely grown (flax, hemp, etc) in the fields.

14. Dinan and the banks of the Rance

The old port at Dinan, the more modern one at le Lyvet, and the wide river between make a fine setting for this classic walk. The first part is fairly energetic, climbing along the high wooded cliffs of the east bank, but you can afford to do justice to a meal at le Lyvet, as the way home is just a gentle stroll along the towpath on the opposite side.

Grade: Strenuous (at least in parts!)

Distance: 14km (8¾ miles)

Time: 4½ hours

Map: IGN TOP 25 1116 ET

Start and finish: The Gothic bridge at the port of Dinan

How to get there: The port is south-east of the town – follow signs to Lanvallay. There is parking on the quayside on both banks of the river. It is also possible to park in one of the many designated places outside the town walls and walk down to the port.

Refreshment: The port and town of Dinan have restaurant facilities of all kinds. There are also bars and restaurants beside the river at le Lyvet.

Notes: The first part of this walk includes some fairly steep climbs up banks which can be muddy. Good footwear is recommended, along with a certain agility! Although the east bank is wooded, the towpath on the west is unshaded – you may need protection from the sun on a hot day. You could carry fluid, but it is possible to get drinks – and food – at le Lyvet.

Waymarking: The route is waymarked in yellow throughout.

Introduction

North of Dinan, the Rance cuts a surprisingly deep estuary on the last leg of its journey to the sea. Arriving there, it now meets the famous barrage, which makes use of one of the highest rises of tide in the world to produce electric power. Once those tides swept all the way up to Dinan, but when the Ille-et-Rance Canal was created almost 200 years ago, the river was dammed at le Lyvet, and thenceforth Dinan became an inland port. The old buildings along the quayside date from its seafaring days.

From the riverside, Dinan is to be seen in all its medieval splendour. Clinging to the rocky cliffs high above, the ancient ramparts encircle an imposing jumble of roofs, towers and spires piercing the skyline. Inside the ramparts, the town is just as impressive, with street after street of astonishingly well-preserved buildings from half a millennium ago. Be warned – in summer those cobbled streets can be thronged with many admirers. But in winter the town goes about its day-to-day business seemingly oblivious of its antiquity, and you can feel you have discovered it for yourself.

From the town, a winding narrow street leads under the ramparts to descend to the port. The old buildings here are garlanded with flowers in summertime and an interesting diversity of craft line the quay. An old 'Gothic' bridge crosses the river and it is from here that the walk starts. The route was originally devised by the Auberge de Jeunesse (Youth Hostel) at Dinan, and, as such, there is an element of adventure about it.

The way initially follows the right bank, taking a detour to cross a marshy swamp that was once a meander of the river, obliterated in the creation of the canal. The steep bank following gives you a first taste of the terrain to come, but your efforts are rewarded by the lovely stone village and superb views at the top. The path continues, alternately dipping to the shore and climbing up the wooded cliffs. On the way you pass a viewpoint known as the *Saut à la Puce* (Flea's Leap), a château, several villages, a nature reserve and an iron age hill fort. At le Lyvet you return to the river to walk beside the port, where huge sea-going yachts strangely mingle with narrowboats destined for the canal trip south. The restaurant beside the river bridge looks tempting!

The way home along the towpath is easy – no climbs, and not even the excitement of finding the way. Particularly on a Sunday, it may seem that half the population of Dinan along with their grandmothers, dogs and children have decided to join you – not to mention the evidently thriving jogging club and the many oarsmen on the river. But this only adds interest to the walk, and soon the high ramparts of the town appear before you, heralding a return to the quayside.

The Walk

1. Leave the Gothic bridge and walk downstream along the east bank, with the river on your left. The road ends at the *station d'epuration*, and behind these buildings, the path splits into three. Take the centre route between high earthen banks (look for the yellow flash on a tree) and then bear round to the right beside a field. Continuing, the path skirts the bed of the old river and then crosses it on a sort of wooden causeway. The first energetic climb follows, as you make your way up log steps set in the bank beneath the trees. On meeting a high wall, turn left to reach the road.

2. Here a wooden signpost informs you that le Lyvet is a mere 5km away. Before following it to the left, you may care to cast a glance at the entrance to the Château de Grillemont a few metres along to the right – you will see its imposing other face across the river as you return. Now continuing towards le Lyvet, you soon come to the hamlet of Landeboulou, and after passing its château, turn left at a T-junction. Where this road bends left, take the path on the right, again waymarked. The path drops down through woodland

Old houses beside the port at Dinan

to the river and then follows beside it under the trees. This part is not exactly a highway and some agility is needed to negotiate the tree roots. Soon you arrive at a little valley and cross the stream on a wooden plank bridge. This is the site of Port Josselin, where in Roman times, the river could be forded to reach the village of Taden. Now following the waymarks away from the river, climb a steep bank on log steps. Continue following the waymarks, and soon you are walking high above the river with a field on your right. After 10 minutes or so of this, a wooden sign announces that you have arrived at the *Saut à la Puce,* where there are fine views down the river. The path descends again quite steeply from here, heading back into the trees and soon reaching a tarmacked road.

3. Now turn left, and immediately right to cross a bridge over the Ruisseau Sainte-Geneviève. Bear left behind the house to where the track ends beside the riverside reeds. Now turn right, and crossing some rocks, climb steeply up the bank again. This time the climb is only short, and reaching a track you follow the yellow waymarks to the left. The path continues under the trees and then descends to yet another valley, the Val Orieux. Here the stream is crossed on a little plank bridge, after which the path bears left, uphill. It is fortunately well-waymarked. Cross beneath a barrier (a log nailed between trees) and reaching a broad track, keep ahead, still climbing. Shortly, pass signs on the left telling you that you have reached the site of the *Éperon Barré*, an Iron Age fort in a commanding position high above the river. The deep ditches were the part of the rear defences of the fort. Now continue on the broad track, which bears right and then shortly left to enter the village of le Châtelier.

From here there is a fine view of the harbour at le Lyvet – to see it, take the first road on the left (Chemin de la Cale) and then the first on the right. But to continue on the walk, keep ahead through the village and turn left as the road swings to the right (Impasse du Val). Shortly bear right on a cobbled track through a tunnel under the bushes. This leads to yet another little valley, where this time the stream is crossed on stepping-stones. Another fairly steep climb takes you out of the trees and on to a tarmacked road.

4. Turn left on the road, from which there are soon fine views. Ahead the railway bridge spans the curving river while nearer to you is the port at le Lyvet and beyond it, the barrage. Keep ahead on the road until about 100 metres before its junction. Here take the waymarked sunken track on the left, which leads down between fields to le Lyvet. At its end, turn left on the road to reach the waterside. Now turn right and walk beside the harbour as far as the road bridge, passing a fine assortment of boats and some interesting possibilities for refreshment. At one time you were allowed to cross the barrage itself – you can still see yellow waymarks – but now it is shut off and you must cross the river on the road bridge. At the far side, walk down behind the lock-keeper's house to join the towpath.

5. It is now quite simple to find your way home. Continuing on the towpath, at about the half-way point you will pass close to Taden, a village built on an old Gallo-Roman site close to the ford over the river. The riverside here has become a popular picnic spot with tables provided. Display boards tell you that this is a site of special ornithological interest with all manner of winter visitors to this particularly wide stretch of water. In about half an hour after this, you will get that view of the façade of the Château de Grillemont peering down from its rocky height across the water, and shortly after, the ramparts of Dinan loom ahead as you approach the port again.

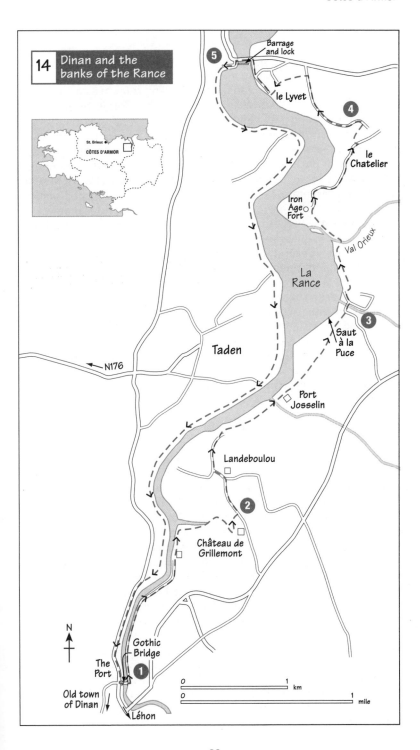

14 Dinan and the banks of the Rance

Barrage and lock
5
le Lyvet
4
le Chatelier
Iron Age Fort
Val Orieux
La Rance
Saut à la Puce
3
Taden
N176
Port Josselin
Landeboulou
2
Château de Grillemont
0   1 km
0   1 mile
N
Gothic Bridge
The Port
1
Old town of Dinan
Léhon

More Walks in the Area

The other classic walk from Dinan – again popular with the local inhabitants – is a walk along the Rance in the opposite direction, to the village of Léhon with its ancient abbey and ruins of a castle. It is a short walk of about 3km each way (from the Gothic bridge), and passes a little island and a lock on the river.

For exploration further afield, the Office du Tourisme in Dinan has produced an inexpensive pack of walks entitled *Randonnées en Pays de Dinan*. This pack contains enough to provide you with a lifetime of holiday walks in the region – coast, forest, river and lake are here in multiple representations. If you just settle for the one leaflet relating to the *District de Dinan* you will have 14 walks on various themes. As there is no text with these walks (no problems with language!), all rely on their good waymarking.

And finally, for a truly excellent walk, you could consider following the Grande Randonnée (GR34C) along the west bank of the Rance to Dinard. This is a lot easier than it sounds, as there is a good bus service to the villages en route – the Office du Tourisme can give you details. The whole distance is 40km (25 miles), and the route is easy to follow from the IGN map (1116 ET), with the usual excellent waymarking of a GR. The views across the estuary are magnificent and on the way you pass several tide mills, many fine beaches and the pretty villages of le Minihic and la Richardais with their harbours. Finally, there is the famous power station at the Barrage de la Rance, to which you can make a short (and free!) visit.

Places of interest nearby

A visit to the old town of Dinan is a must. From the port, walk up the steep Rue du Jerzual and through the arch under the ramparts – this itself is one of the most delightful streets in the town. Alternatively, leave your car in one of the many parking areas outside the walls and enter through a gate – but take note of which one, as the maze of medieval streets within can be quite confusing. Once inside, it is best to wander at will – it is not a town where there are important sites to visit, and there is no 'Town Trail'. It is simply amazing to find such an array of seemingly perfect medieval buildings. Close to the centre of town (and the Office du Tourisme) is the *Tour d'Horloge* with its deafening 500-year-old bell. If you have any trouble finding it, just wait for the hour! It is possible to climb to the top of this tower from which there is a magnificent view of the town, the river and surrounding countryside. More excellent views can be had from walking round the ramparts – on the east side of the town, these lead to the *Jardin Anglais* and the *Tour Ste-Cathérine*, which looks out over the river and port below.

The nearby town of Dinard, with its confusingly similar name, offers something totally different. A one-time watering hole of the world's rich and famous who came to enjoy the sea air and mild climate, it retains today many of their exotic residences. Its clientèle, more mixed nowadays, can still take pleasure in the three sandy beaches and subtropical vegetation. In short, it is a most pleasant place to take the family for a day by the sea – but you might also like to visit the curious little *Musée du Site Balnéaire*, which records scenes from its former life, along with displays on changing styles of the bathing costume.

Just south of Dinard is the barrage across the river, and at its centre, the *Usine Marémotrice de la Rance*. This tidal hydro-electric power station makes use of one of the highest rises of tide in the world (13.5 m) to generate about 8 percent of Brittany's energy requirement. You can walk along the dam, be impressed by the swirling currents and take a free tour of the power station.

The towns of Dinan, Dinard and St Malo are all seen at their best when approached from the water and in summer there are boat trips on the Rance linking all three. The Office du Tourisme can give you information.

15. 'Chaos' in the Gorges of the Corong

Through the high moorland plateau of the Corong, the Rivière de Follezou has cut a deep wooded gorge. In the riverbed there are huge rounded boulders, made smooth by wind and rain over millions of years – your way lies across them.

Grade: Moderate (with a scramble across the boulders!)

Distance: 5km (3 miles)

Time: 1½ hours or thereabouts

Map: IGN Série Bleue 0717 E

Start and finish: Menhir de Quélénec

How to get there: The Menhir de Quélénec stands just south of the D20, about 16km east of Carhaix-Plougier. It is about 5km east of the village of Locarn. There is a small parking area adjacent to the road.

Refreshment: Quite simply – none! But there is an interesting bar/restaurant, the Relais du Corong, in Locarn.

Notes: This route has now been made into a *Sentier de Découverte* with its own 'bird of prey' logo (actually a hen harrier) and numbered stopping places. The guide book that accompanies the route (French only) tells you of the geographical and geological features of the area, and details some of the wildlife. It can be obtained from the smart new Maison du Patrimoine in Locarn – see below. Here we follow the route for its own sake – and you will see that you reach the numbered features in reverse order. The walk is easy and can be tackled in trainers, at least in summer. Non-slip soles are a must for crossing the rocks. It doesn't take very long, so you might like to combine it with a picnic at the menhir and/or another walk in the area – see the suggestions below. Take binoculars for the views – and don't forget to look out for the otters!

Waymarking: The route is waymarked with blue flashes throughout, to which have been added the blue and yellow markers.

Introduction

The plateau of Huelgoat spreads out across northern Brittany, a remote and wild plateau of granite schist, an easterly continuation of the Monts d'Arrée. At one time, all this land was covered by forest, but since Romans times much of this has been felled. Its replacement is *la lande* – the moorland – a windswept and untamed land of gorse, bracken and heather which has a beauty of its own

Through this plateau the rivers have cut deep, often wooded valleys, with waterfalls and landslides of boulders that have rolled down the rocky slopes aeons ago. The gorges of Corong and those of Toul Goulic are quite spectacular. In these lonely rivers the water is pure enough to attract otters – they are very shy creatures and not easily seen, but you could look out for their footprints and droppings by the riverside. You may also see the hen harriers – grey with black wing tips – circling in the skies above the moorland. Although not on the usual tourist trail, this is certainly a land that will appeal to walkers.

It seems that this high plateau also had its attractions for prehistoric man – the walk starts from the Menhir de Quélénec, which looks out over a wild moorland valley. The site is very picturesque and there are picnic tables and a display board. From here, the path to the gorge crosses an attractive plantation of pines before dipping to the river. When you first meet it, the Follezou is flowing quietly enough through the trees, but soon it is tumbling and cascading beside you in a very energetic fashion, before completely disappearing under a huge pile of rounded polished boulders, filling the whole valley – truly a 'chaos'! The Breton interpretation of this scene is that a passing giant emptied the gravel from his shoe here – but another explanation is that the rocky sides of this valley are fissured, allowing rain water to seep in and split off huge fragments, which then become rounded by erosion. The route actually crosses these boulders – and for this you need to be reasonably agile – before climbing out of the gorge through the woods. The way back lies along the edge of the *Landes de Locarn* itself – now protected moorland with rare plant and bird life. If you want to learn more about it before you set out, visit the Maison du Patrimoine in Locarn.

Ruisseau de Follezou

93

The Walk

1. With the parking for the menhir behind you, cross the road and take the broad grassy track almost opposite. Soon you are walking between plantations of Norway Spruce with the open moorland on the horizon. The path bends left, and you are in wild country with gorse to the left and woods to the right. Rushing water can be heard ahead, and the path turns into the woods to cross the river at the site of a former water-mill. On the far side of the river, bear left and follow the blue flashes on the path through the trees.

2. On reaching the tarmacked road, turn left, and then shortly, below the parking area, bear right, following the waymarks. Continuing ahead, you cross a stream and then follow beside a low wall of old stones above the River Follezou, on a most attractive downhill path through the woods. Rocky outcrops loom to the right while the river bounces and skips over cascades of boulders to the left. After a while the whole valley is full of boulders, and the river has disappeared. Now look out for a blue arrow on a tree directing you to turn left across this rocky chaos. You can easily be deceived, as there are also blue markers on the path continuing beside the river – but someone has thoughtfully (and rather garishly!) marked the turn with a spot of iridescent pink.

3. Clamber across the boulders to reach a path on the far side that climbs uphill through the trees. This woodland was once the home of charcoal burners and their families. Traces of their slow-burning stacks still remain in the undergrowth. After about 100 metres, at the cross-tracks, turn right and continue to follow the blue flashes on a twisting path up the side of the valley. Emerging on a sunken lane, turn left and keep ahead to meet a stony road at a car park.

4. The high moorland is now before you, but you turn right and follow the fence along the edge of it. The path descends a little and then climbs with increasingly fine distant views as you go. At the height you can see the Monts d'Arrée to the west (can you see the chapel on the top of Ménez-Mikel? – see Walk 24!) and, south of these hills, the Montagnes Noires. The path goes on to pass another menhir and then runs along the side of sand quarries where swallows nest in summer. On reaching the road, turn left and continue along it for about 300 metres to return to the Menhir de Quélénec.

More Walks in the Area

There are several other 'gorge-walks' in the area. The nearest is a short walk in the Gorges de Toul Goulic, a few kilometres away to the east, off the D87 between the villages of Trémargat and Lanrivain. Here the

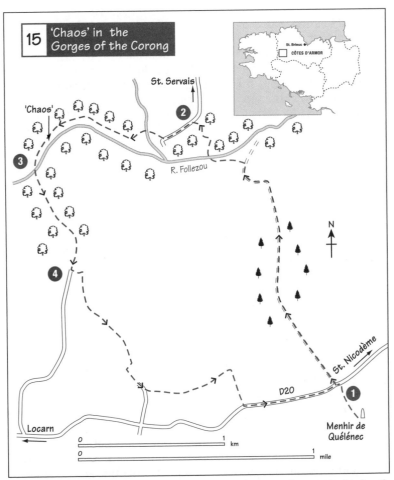

St. Servais

'Chaos'

2

3

R. Follezou

N

4

St. Nicodème

D20

1

Locarn

Menhir de Quélénec

St. Brieuc
CÔTES D'ARMOR

0 _____ 1 km

0 _____ 1 mile

River Blavet disappears to an underground chasm beneath the boulders – quite spectacular! Farther to the east are the Gorges du Daoulas (see Walk 6) – a few megaliths are thrown in as well on this walk. Still farther east (approx.45km from the Corong) are the Gorges de Poulancre. A waymarked walk from the pretty floral village of Saint-Gilles-Vieux-Marché takes you through them. And for yet another 'chaos' in a wooded valley, head for Rostrenen, where the Office du Tourisme should be able to give you details of *La Boucle de Restouarc'h*. Along with the pretty valley of the Doré, this walk offers some interesting villages, an old railway track and the fine chapel at Locmaria.

For a valley walk with something a little different, you are only about 12km from a short (4.5km) waymarked walk taking you past the remains of an old Roman aqueduct. The walk starts from Roscoat (head for Locarn, Maël-Carhaix and then Kerogiou where you turn left) and features a stream and water-mills along with the vestiges of the aqueduct, which are identified by green boards. Details of the walk can be obtained from Tourist Information at Rostrenen or Mûr-de-Bretagne – or you can chance your luck and follow the yellow waymarks uphill from the road junction at Roscoat, turning right across the field at the top of the incline.

And finally, for something a little educational as well, there is a waymarked 4km circuit from le Moustoir (on the N164 just east of Carhaix-Plougier). This is a very pretty short walk, again through a wooded valley, where trees and plants have been named – in both French and Breton. There are also several attractive picnic sites on the walk – ask for details at an Office du Tourisme.

Places of interest nearby

The Nantes-Brest Canal is about 20km away, just south of the N164. A good spot from which to view it is reached by turning off that road at la Pie, where there is a picnic site beside the canal. The canal was built by Napoleon as an inland cut for his fleet, thus avoiding the incursions of the British at sea. Since the damming of the River Blavet in the 1920s, the centre portion of the canal between Carhaix-Plougier and Pontivy is now navigable by nothing greater than a canoe. But its towpath makes a good walk, and from la Pie you can walk east towards Glomel, passing several disused locks along a peaceful reed-fringed stretch of waterway.

Carhaix-Plougier itself, though a major crossroads in Roman times, is now not a town of very great note. You may well be seeking the Office du Tourisme here, in which case you will also see the town's most remarkable building, the Maison de Sénéchal, in which it is housed. Carved figures and statuettes adorn its16th century façade. The statue in the square is of a soldier with the grand name of Théophile-Malo Corret, la Tour d'Auvergne! He managed a distinguished career in the Napoleonic army together with studies and publications on the Celtic languages.

South-west of Carhaix-Plougier (turn right off the D769 at Port-de-Carhaix – where you can again see the Nantes-Brest Canal) is the Kerbreudeur Calvary, dating from the 15th century and thought to be the oldest in Brittany. For another typically Breton elaborate calvary, continue along this road for 2km to the village of St-Hernin, with its fine parish close.

A path through the beechwoods

Morbihan

16. Beside the River Ellé at le Faouët

Le Faouët is well-named, *faou* being an old Breton word for a beech tree. This walk climbs through the beech woods beside the 'chaos' of the tumbling River Ellé to reach the 15th century stone chapel of Ste. Barbe, perched on rock high above the river.

Grade: Moderate

Distance: 12km (7½ miles)

Time: 3 hours

Map: IGN Série Bleue 0719 0 – but the Office du Tourisme in le Faouët stocks an inexpensive walking map of the area including other marked circuits

Start and Finish: The town square at le Faouët.

How to get there: Le Faouët lies just off the D769, some 40km north of Lorient. All roads lead to the town square, where there is plenty of parking.

Refreshment: Eating places of all kinds are to be found around the square – although the choice is more limited out of season.

Notes: This is not a particularly difficult walk, but there is a short scramble up rock to the viewpoint over the valley. Trainers should be adequate in summer, but out of season walking boots would be preferable. The walk is largely in the woods, making it very suitable for a hot day – take fluid with you.

Waymarking: The route is waymarked throughout with signposts, yellow flashes on trees and rocks, and an occasional walking man figurine.

Introduction

The countryside around le Faouët is termed the *Pays de Roi Morvan* after the Breton King Morvan who was here defeated in battle against the Franks in the 9th century. The Bretons were always a rebellious crew, and Morvan was just one of a succession of leaders who physically opposed Frankish domination. The land that now bears his name must be one of the most attractive – and little known – parts of Brittany. This is the Argoat, the forested country of the interior, and here among rushing rivers and wooded hillsides it seems that every village possesses a medieval building of some note. Chapels, manors, halls, abbeys and water-mills are scattered liberally across the rolling landscape.

Le Faouët itself is a most pleasant small town, and boasts a vast covered market hall, dating from the 16th century, set in an attractive tree-lined square.

Outside the town are villages with remarkable medieval chapels, magnificent woods of beech and oak, and a steep valley where the little River Ellé tumbles over a 'chaos' of boulders in its rocky bed. This

Chaos of the Ellé in autumn

is fine walking country, and the local rambling group has waymarked several interesting circuits in the area. On their recommendation, this walk combines the best of them – and will almost certainly tempt you to try others.

The walk leaves from the town square, and before long you are enjoying those fine woods. Reaching the bridge over the Ellé, you climb steadily beside the rushing river on a path meandering through the trees to emerge at a rocky view point high above the valley. This is a walk which is excellent at any time of year, but on a sunny Autumn day the colours are quite stunning, the burning amber of the beeches contrasting with the deep greens of the undergrowth and mossy rocks. Dropping down again from the viewpoint, you pass the pumping station at the head of the valley before doubling back along its top edge with fine views all the way. Plunging back into the woods you come upon an ancient fountain and then the ornate, gothic-style chapel of Ste Barbe itself, clinging to the rock below the rim. It seems a strange place for such a fine chapel, but the story goes that in 1489, Jean le Toulbodou, a local landowner, was out hunting here when a severe storm broke. Lightening split the rock face beside him, and in terror he prayed to Ste Barbe, to take care of him. She did – and in gratitude he built this grand edifice. Should you, too, be here in a storm (apparently this place attracts lightning!) you are advised to invøke the blessing of Ste. Barbe by tolling the bell in its house at the top of the steps – but you will need to be strong to move it. From the chapel, an old paved pilgrims' path through the woods takes you back to the town below.

The Walk

1. Leave the central square via a narrow road from the middle of the north side, opposite the covered market – the Rue des Halles. Cross the road at the top and continue ahead on the Chemin de Ste. Barbe. Soon you are on a lovely wide high-banked path beneath the trees that leads you down to a tunnel under the expressway. Here you meet the first of the fine wooden signposts that mark the forest paths. Cross under the expressway and on the far side turn immediately right following the direction of the *Circuit du Chaos*. This path continues for about 500 metres through the woodland above and parallel to the expressway. The path then clearly bends left away from the road and after a further 300 metres or so brings you to a fork. Here do not take the path left into the wood, but go straight ahead and descend to the road beside the river bridge.

2. Walk along the road, and just before the bridge, take the track on the left which is signed with a yellow flash on the *Circuit des Chapelles*. As you approach an old mill, the track forks and you bear left above the mill, following the signs. Continuing uphill on this track through the woods another signpost is soon reached, and here you turn right following the direction of the *Circuit du Chaos*. Winding your way through the waymarked trees, you arrive at the riverside. The path from here beside the rocky river is quite delightful, and you follow it for some 3km, climbing gently all the while. At one point some big rocks bar the way, but the yellow flashes direct you to keep left and climb them. A fine view across the valley awaits you at the top – it's also a good spot for a picnic. Descending again on the waymarked path you once more follow the river, which after a while becomes calmer, while the path beside it widens as it passes through a plantation of pines. The path then leaves the river and climbs again to reach the white buildings of the pumping station.

3. Just after the pumping station, the waymarks direct you to the right, but now you ignore them. Instead, continue ahead on the road which doubles back as it climbs above the pine wood. In about 400 metres, after passing the stone buildings of a farm on the right, another wooden signpost is seen. Turn left, following the pointer to the *Circuit du Chaos* back down into the wood. The path now runs high on the side of the valley, and, after again turning uphill, emerges on the top with views all around. Gorse and bracken line the path and soon a fingerpost directs you through them to a viewpoint. Continuing again, you soon ignore a path to the Ellé going off to the left and then reach a tarmacked road at a small hamlet.

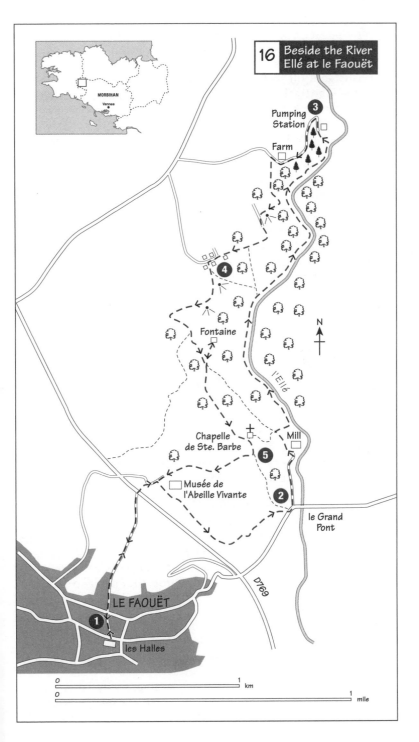

16 Beside the River Ellé at le Faouët

4. After passing between farm buildings, turn left following another *Circuit du Chaos* signpost. Passing more viewpoints, you arrive in about 500 metres at a major track junction. Here the *Circuit du Chaos* goes off to the right uphill, but you leave it and follow instead the track ahead towards *Ste. Barbe*. Almost immediately, at another fork, follow the direction of *Fontaine* (now ignoring *Ste. Barbe*) A further 250 metres or so along this track brings you to another fork with a broad path going uphill to the right. This is the Pilgrims' Path leading up to the chapel – but, look behind you! The Pilgrims' Path continues downhill to reach the *Fontaine,* a spring where clear bubbling water arises in a well-head dating from 1708.

Return now on the Pilgrim's Path where soon the grey eerie bulk of the Chapel of Ste. Barbe appears through the trees as you climb. Through the archway, steps lead uphill to the bell house on the edge of a flat plateau with distant views. The custodian's house is nearby and at holiday times it should be possible to view the interior of the chapel where there are fine stained glass windows.

5. When you are ready to leave, walk along the edge of the field away from the bell house. Continue ahead past the barrier at the wide gap in the wall and alongside the next field. Stones begin to appear in your path, and very soon you are on a cobbled track dipping into the woods. This is again the Pilgrim's Path, which then descends quite steeply and, just before the express-way, passes some converted farm buildings which now house the *Musée de lAbeille Vivante* – a bee and ant museum. The picnic tables outside look inviting, but if you prefer to eat in town, keeping ahead and retracing your steps under the expressway will quickly return you to the square at le Faouët.

More Walks in the Area

From the Office du Tourisme at le Faouët, you can obtain a map of the region, showing 10 waymarked routes. For each of these there is an accompanying free leaflet – in French – giving directions, a sketch map, and lots of information. Even if you cannot manage the French, it should be possible to follow these routes from the maps and excellent waymarking. The *Circuit de Saint-Sébastien* (10km), following the valley of the River Ellé, is most attractive. Another choice would be the *Circuit de Diarnelez* (10.5km), which visits the ancient manor of that name above the valley of the River Inam. Also, the circuit that visits the chapels of both Ste. Barbe and St Fiacre is a very popular one.

To the east of le Faouët and the Ellé is another pretty valley, that of the River Scorff. At Guémené-sur-Scorff there are again waymarked circuits and free leaflets for these are obtainable from the Office du

Tourisme – or the *Mairie*, out of season. The route that climbs through the wooded valley of the Scorff to St Auny is most picturesque and passes chapels, ancient villages, water-mills and many fine viewpoints. This attractive part of Brittany seems quite unknown – and is ideal for discovering on foot.

Places of interest nearby

If you are interested in ancient chapels, you must surely start at St Fiacre, just south of le Faouët. This 15th century chapel, with fine stained glass windows, is best known for its magnificent carved and painted rood screen, depicting in the most graphic form the seven deadly sins. At St Nicholas, just to the east, is another fine rood screen, while more medieval gruesomeness is revealed in the remarkable 15th century wall paintings at Kernascléden (10km east). There are more notable chapels at le Croisty and St Tugdual, St Caradac-Trégomel and Berné – and at Langonnet there is an abbey with an original chapter house dating from the 13th century. The whole area is dotted with these buildings, and an area ma p *'Pays de Roi Morvan'* from the Office du Tourisme will give you a good idea of where to look for them.

For more active pursuits, there are lakes for sailing and swimming at Priziac, Langoëlan, Plouray and Langonnet, and the Ellé and the Scorff are great rivers for fishing. South of Meslan is wild country known as the Roches du Diable where the Ellé crashes through a wooded gorge with fine viewpoints. More walks are possible, along with fishing, mountain biking, canoeing and other activities.

17. The Golden Cliffs of Pénestin

The little resort of Pénestin sits at the southern edge of Brittany where the wide River Vilaine meets the sea. This walk is one of contrasts – high cliffs along the sea coast, salt marshes in the estuary, and inland, the *bocage*, the ancient Breton countryside with its high-banked tracks.

Grade: Easy

Distance: 13km (8¼ miles)

Time: 3½ hours continuous walking

Map: IGN TOP25 1022 OT

Start and Finish: The Office du Tourisme just south of the town centre at Pénestin.

How to get there: Pénestin is on the Atlantic coast between Vannes and La Baule. Follow the N165 east from Vannes and leave at La Roche Bernard (S.P. Pénestin). At the roundabout just before town, turn left. The Office du Tourisme is on the right and there is plenty of parking outside.

Refreshment: There are several bars and restaurants in Pénestin – with particular emphasis on *Fruits de Mer*. If not dining out, you can always take some home from the *Poissonerie* in the town.

Notes: This is an easy walk, quite suitable for trainers in dry weather. Extending your walk along the estuary about a kilometre will bring you to the port of Tréhiguer, where you can visit the mussel museum and find refreshment to sustain you for the short journey home. Most of the route is exposed, so you should think of protection from the sun on a hot day, and carry fluid with you.

Waymarking: Along the coast and estuary the route follows the Grande Randonnée and so is waymarked with flashes of white on red. Elsewhere there are occasional green waymarks.

Introduction

Pénestin is an out-of-the-way sort of place. It is cut off from the rest of Brittany by the wide estuary of the Vilaine and from the land to the south and east by the great marsh of the Brière. A little farther along the coast is the modern resort of La Baule, but its sophistication has not rubbed off on Pénestin. This is a pleasant and unspoilt little town which, despite some very fine beaches, has rarely found its way into the guide books.

It must have been something of a shock to the inhabitants when, at the end of the 19th century, Pénestin was found to be sitting on gold. A gold mine was opened near the town, but the venture was short-lived, the returns were poor, and at the time of the First World War the mine was closed down. It remains only in name – the nearby popular beach is the Plage de la Mine d'Or, where, interestingly enough, the sandstone cliffs at sunset glow with the colour of the precious metal. Along

Skeletons of boats in the harbour of Camaret (walk 25)

Clifftop path, Pénestin (walk 17)

View across Guéhenno from 'Le Mont' (walk 18)

Path through Arthur's Camp (showing ramparts) (walk 20)

Chapel of St Samson (walk 23)

Château de la Hunaudaye (walk 13)

Along the cliffs (walk 26)

Fontaine de la Chapelle Neuve (walk 28)

Across the estuary of the Vilaine, Pénestin

these cliffs, then, the walk sets out, and you have views of the rocky coast and small islands to sea as you go.

Moving onwards, there are more fine beaches before reaching the rocky Pointe de Halguen and the estuary. Oddly, it is the estuary rather than the sea that has supported Pénestin's economy through the ages. For many centuries, sea salt was harvested here, and along the estuary you can still see the rectangular pits where sea water was circulated and evaporated by sun and wind to form the crystals of salt. This all ceased at the end of the 19th century and since then, mussel farming (*la mytiliculture*) has become an important industry. The fine quality of the mussels is said to be due to the oxygenated water mingling with the seawater in the estuary. At low tide, look out for rows of *buchots* – the posts where mussels collect. At Tréhiguer, a little farther along the shore (you could extend your walk) the old lighthouse has been converted to house a 'mussel museum', and is well worth a visit. The route returns to Pénestin on quiet roads and sunken lanes, past a manor house and over a hill with a view. Once back in town, there are several good sea-food restaurants where you could check out the quality of those mussels.

The Walk

1. From the Office du Tourisme, walk down the road away from the town to the roundabout. Here turn right to reach the Sports Hall. Walking behind the Sports Hall, you reach a path which runs

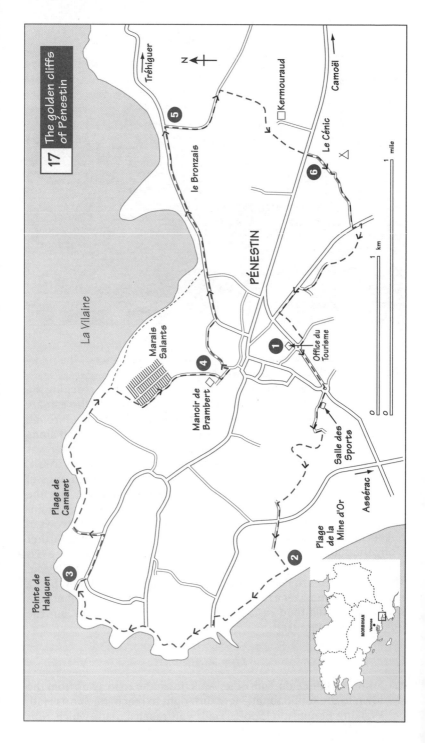

between the football pitch and the tennis courts. At the end of the football pitch, turn right on the grassy track. In about 100 metres (just around the corner), bear left at junction of sunken tracks, and in about 15 metres, bear left again at another junction. The track you are now on bears right and then passes to the right of the houses to reach a tarmacked road. Cross this to the track directly opposite. At the fork in front of a house, bear left – you can actually see a green waymark here! Soon you arrive at the cliff-top path. To the left you can see the Plage de la Mine d'Or with its golden cliffs, and beyond it, a rocky promontory with a little island (Île de Bel Air). Much farther out is the larger Île Dumet.

2. Turn right on the cliff-top path. Below you is a glorious sandy beach, ahead is the Pointe de Halguen at the mouth of the estuary and behind it, the whole south coast of Morbihan. Gorse and pines line the path as you go. At the end of the cliffs, you find yourself in dunes above rocky outcrops and, keeping to the coastal path, continue around an attractive curving bay. As you reach the point, the waymarks direct you away from the coast around the fence of the building at the end. Returning to the coast, a seat under the pines gives a fine view across the mouth of the estuary.

3. On reaching a small road coming down to another little beach (Plage de Halguen), turn right following the green arrow. Continue bearing left at the top and then follow the road for about 300 metres, to where a road on the left takes you down to the Plage de Camaret – there is a green flash on the telegraph pole. This is another attractive little beach, after which some more climbing leads you to the Plage de Menard. Here you are in a wide grassy area beside the estuary. Ahead are the *marais salants* – the old salt pits – and if you fancy an adventure it is possible to pick your way between them and the sea. But the safer route turns inland here along a broad grassy track between pines and gorse. Waymarks direct you to bear left and you follow along behind the salt marsh, crossing a little bridge over an entrant stream. The path approaches the town and reaches a junction with the old Manoir de Brambert on the right.

4. Turn left here and shortly, at a T-junction, left again following the colour flashes on the Rue de Lienne. At the end of this road, turn left on the wider road. On your left is a pleasant area of pines and picnic tables alongside the estuary – you could choose to leave the road and walk on the far side of them instead. Again on the road, continue through the village of Le Bronzais and then turn right on the Route de Berniguet – there is a green flash on the corner. But if you wish to visit the village and port of Tréhiguer (mussel museum, bar/restaurant), it is just 1km farther along the road.

5. The Route de Berniguet bears sharp left, and then slightly right. At this bend, where the road begins to climb again, take the track on the right between high banks – there should be a green waymark at its entrance. Continue on the tree-lined track with good views of the estuary to the right. Ignore all side tracks (the waymarks have mysteriously disappeared) until you pass a lake on the right and see farm buildings ahead (Manoir de Kermouraud). Now keep to the right-hand track which winds round and uphill to come out at a tarmacked road. Here continue ahead to reach the main road shortly.

6. Cross directly over the main road to the road opposite. This skirts a campsite on the left and descends, bearing right to a road junction. Here turn left, and after about 30 metres, turn right on a track where again there is a green waymark. The track joins a road beside some new housing and this road continues, bearing right to reach a main road. Turn left towards the church, but just before the end of the road, turn left on a track called the Chemin de Lavoir. Bearing right at the end of this brings you to the main road where the Office du Tourisme is just opposite.

More Walks in the Area

The Office du Tourisme at Pénestin stocks maps and also an inexpensive small booklet of walks in the area which is well worth having. If you have enjoyed coastal walking, try the walk south along the cliffs following the *Sentier Côtier* as far as the *Baie du Bile* (approx. 7km from Pénestin). At high tide this is a very pretty bay, at low tide it is a hive of activity with shellfish farmers going about their business in the oyster and mussel beds.

A short circular waymarked walk from Camoël (about 6km east) will take you past the attractive port at the *Barrage d'Arzal*, the dam which cuts off the tidal portion of the Vilaine. The Office du Tourisme again has details.

The navigable part of the River Vilaine has a walkable towpath beside it for much of the way – it connects with the Rance north of Rennes, so you could actually walk to Dinan. There are also many interesting circular walks along its valley. A Topoguide (*Vallée de la Vilaine et de l'Oust – Ref. 077*) containing 50 of these is published by the FFRP and is available in most bookshops locally – the maps in this Topoguide are good, but a certain knowledge of French would be helpful for the text. This Topoguide also contains the route of a Grande Randonnée, the GR 39, which approximately follows the Vilaine from Rennes to the sea. Grandes Randonnées are always well waymarked, and sections of this one can easily be followed using a taxi from start or finish – ask the Office du Tourisme to help you with arrangements.

Since you are in this area, a visit to the Brière National Park (south-east of Pénestin) is a must. This is an ancient land of marshes and canals where peat-cutting and reed gathering are traditional occupations. Walking is possible here only between June and September, but there are several waymarked paths (routes available from the Tourist Offices at La Chapelle des Marais and St Joachim) and the strange light across these marshes makes walking a magical experience.

Places of interest nearby

The port, restaurant and mussel museum at Tréhiguer have already been mentioned in the text. At least go along and collect a few recipes.

Should you be wondering exactly how the sea salt was collected from those pits along the estuary, there are two small museums that can help you – the *Maison des Paludiers* at Salle near Guérande (about 25km south of Pénestin) and the nearby *Musée des Marais Salants* at Batz-sur-Mer. Salt is still harvested from the bay south of Guérande, where you can see a vast patchwork of salt pans and drainage channels, much beloved by wading birds of all kinds.

If you feel like exploring the Vilaine by boat rather than on foot, there are daily trips up that river from the barrage at Arzal. Everything from a simple trip to a four-hour dinner cruise by candlelight is on offer.

To the south and east of Pénestin is the *Parc Naturel Régional de Brière*, a vast area of marshland and reeds crossed by canals (mentioned also in the 'More Walks' section). Here several 'ports' offer you the opportunity to hire one of the local flat-bottomed boats and take yourself off into the wilderness for the day. If you are afraid of getting lost, you can opt for a guided trip instead. It is truly an area of outstanding natural beauty, but there are other tourist attractions in the form of many preserved old houses and villages in the local style. Call at the Office du Tourisme at La Chapelle des Marais for more information.

18. Guéhenno and the mills of the Sedon Valley.

The Sedon Valley is renowned for its water-mills, although most of them have now been converted to private residences. This walk passes a few of them – and starts from the village of Guéhenno, famous for its ornate calvary.

Grade: Easy

Distance: 5km (3 miles)

Time: 1½ hours

Map: IGN Série Bleue 0919 E

Start and finish: The church at Guéhenno

How to get there: Guéhenno lies on the D778, about 10km south-west of Josselin. There is a car park beside the main road, close to the church.

Refreshment: There are at least three bar/restaurants in Guéhenno – one is opposite the car park. There is a picnic table in a grassy area on top of le Mont.

Notes: This very easy walk is almost entirely on quiet roads and hard-surfaced tracks, making it a route suitable for pushchairs. Only the very short stretch in front of the Moulin de Château Merlet is a little rough. Unfortunately, the last 500 metres or so is along a road which, although not major, can at times be busy.

Waymarking: The route is waymarked in yellow throughout.

Introduction

The Sedon is only a short river – it arises on the high ground beyond Guéhenno and flows into the River Oust near Josselin. But this is rich and fertile countryside, which has traditionally produced a wealth of cereals. The valley of the Sedon was once said to ring with the *chant des moulins*. The mills here had their heyday in the 19th century when the mill was as important to the community as the manor or the church. Acting as a sort of forum for the village, the mill was the place where deals were struck, arrangements were made and news passed on. The miller himself was a wealthy man and, surprisingly, was usually also a person of learning who could be relied upon for information. By the middle of the 20th century, most of the mills were no longer in use. Some simply fell into ruin, while others were restored as private residences. On the walk you take here, one mill is indeed still functioning – but the water now powers a turbine.

The walk starts from the village of Guéhenno. Although it is a pretty village with many interesting old granite houses, it is renowned chiefly for its calvary. The calvaries of Brittany are famous – each is a scripture lesson in itself, with a myriad of carved stone figures playing out their

Calvary at Guéhenno

biblical roles, all clustered around the crosses of Christ and the two thieves. The calvary at Guéhenno is not one of the most elaborate (that at Guimiliau has more than 200 figures!), but it does have a story. The original, dating from around 1550, was destroyed in the Revolution. The estimates for its repair by professional stone masons were far too great, so, some 60 years later, the local priest and his vicar decided to fix things themselves. They got the people to gather together all the fragments of the old calvary that they could find (it is said the revolutionary soldiers played *boules* with the heads!), reassembled them, re-carved them, and created others. The result was the interesting calvary you can see today – the faces are excellent. Look out for Jesse, the father of David, on the stem of the cross, and Mary Magdalene who caries a shroud. The cockerel, on its pillar in front of the calvary, represents Peter's denial of Christ. Behind the calvary is the ossuary – cast here in the role of Christ's tomb, the entrance guarded by soldiers.

The walk from here is very short and very easy. It is actually a walk you could consider if pushing a pushchair – only about 100 metres of it is on rough ground. On the way you will pass four water mills in various states of repair standing beside the rushing River Sedon in a pretty green valley. But before you reach the river, the walk first leads you to the village of Le Mont – aptly named as it sits on the top of a hill. The highest point is crowned by the Chapelle St Michel (St Michel is the patron saint of high places – you had probably noticed.), and around this are grouped some fine stone houses and a farm. On the far side of the summit, just a little lower than the chapel, is an old windmill. There are good views from here across the rich farmland of the valley and someone has thoughtfully provided a picnic table. You could consider returning at the end of your walk.

The Walk

1. Walk away from the main road with the church on your right-hand side. Opposite the church, on your left, is a board announcing the start of the *Circuit des Moulins*. Coming to the end of the road, cross straight over, following signs to the Chapelle St Michel and yellow waymarks. The road climbs and takes a left-hand corner to reach the top of the hill.

2. After admiring the views and the windmill, bear right around the chapel and continue ahead following the waymarks. The road begins to descend, and reaching a stone farm on the right-hand side, you do not go straight ahead, but turn right down the wide track. On reaching the woodland at the bottom of the hill, the track swings to the left and continues ahead to meet the road.

3. Turn right on the road and cross the stream. Here is the first of your old water-mills. This one was built in 1878 and was working until 1940. Just past the old mill you reach a main road and turn left. The road passes the joining place of two streams and continues uphill. After about 500 metres, you reach a road branching off on the right, signposted to the Moulin de Lemay. This road passes through a farm, after which you have good views across the valley on your left. The partially crumbling old farm across the valley is the Manoir de le Clégrio, which originates from the 17th century. The path now descends to the Moulin de Lemay, the mill with a turbine.

4. The path takes you around the right-hand side of the building and continues under the trees. The stream is on your left, and where the track forks, you turn left to cross it on a wooden bridge (this is actually marked *Propriété Privée*, but underneath has been added *Sauf Circuit des Moulins*). The path now crosses in front of the Moulin du Château Merlin which is undergoing restoration. The mill-wheel was on the far side of the house. The path now comes up to a small road.

5. Turn left on the road and continue through the wooded valley of the Sedon. The road is climbing slightly and passes yet another former mill, the Moulin d'Hurnel. This is now a very fine thatched riverside residence. Keeping ahead, you reach a main road. Cross straight over this to the track opposite – again a track beside woodland and the river. This eventually reaches another road, the D778, at which you turn left to return to Guéhenno.

More Walks in the Area

Just 10km away is Josselin on the Nantes à Brest Canal. This is a particularly attractive stretch and very popular with boaters. It is possible to follow the canal towpath both west and east from Josselin – in both

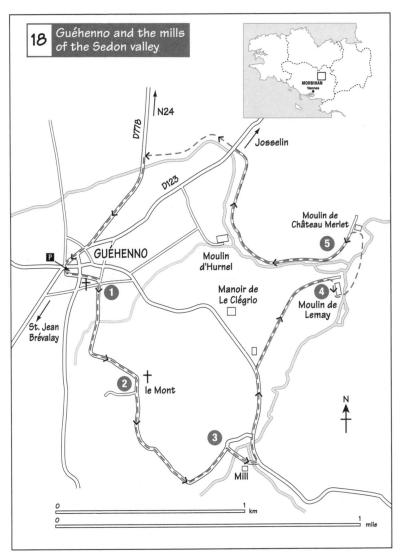

18 Guéhenno and the mills of the Sedon valley

directions the towpath is a wide hard-surfaced track also suitable for pushchairs. Going east there is a very simple circuit you could take if you do not wish to retrace your steps along the towpath – the IGN map above will help you identify it. After following the towpath for about half an hour, just after passing a lock with an island, cross the river bridge and keep ahead up the track. Cross the D4 directly and after about 400 metres take the first road on the right signposted to Gloret. At this hamlet leave the road and keep straight ahead on the track to the hamlet of la Ville Gourdan. Bear right twice to come down to the D4. Turn left on this road, and after 100 metres, right. After a further

100 metres or so, a path leads off through the trees on the left. You now follow above the river, and keeping the castle in view, reach the main road, which then crosses the river in front of the castle

The Office du Tourisme in Josselin stocks a collection of cards entitled *Randonnées au Pays de l'Oust à Brocéliande*. The mapping on these is very clear and the waymarking is good - you should have no difficulty following them. The reverse of each card gives information on points of interest en route.

Two nearby circuits from this collection start from the same point – the Étang du Val Join at Lizio. Since each is short – just 5km – they could easily be combined. The first is a wander over moorland in which you are encouraged to 'learn nothing' but just to employ your senses – no doubt in preparation for the second route, the *Sentier Botanique*. On this walk, every tree and shrub is named and its particular features enumerated. There are even questions on each with answers on the back of the board. You could regard it as a combined lesson in French and botany – or just enjoy the walk! The lake of Val Join itself is well-hidden in an attractive valley, with lakeside parking and picnic tables.

A rather more ambitious circuit of 11km starts from Trégranteur, a few kilometres east of Guéhenno (and south of Josselin). This circuit is charmingly waymarked with little walking figures. The route follows another stretch of the valley of the Sedon where there are yet more water-mills, and returns through the pretty old village of Coët-Bugat and through the forest.

Places of interest nearby

Josselin with its magnificent medieval castle is just a few kilometres away. The building you see today dates from the 14th century. Despite many attacks and attempts to dismantle it, the solid walls and pepper-pot towers are still impressive, reflected in the waters of the River Oust. From the 15th century the castle belonged to the rebellious Rohan family, whose defiant motto was 'Roi ne puis. Prince ne daigne. Rohan suis.' – King I cannot be. I scorn to be a prince. I am a Rohan. In apparent contrast to all this haughtiness, the more recent Rohans became interested in dolls, and their amazing collection from all over the world is on view in the old stables of the castle.

East of Josselin, near Ploërmel, is the Lac du Duc, the largest natural lake in Brittany. Here you can swim, hire boats, enjoy water sports – and walk! The circuit of the lake is 16km – you can pick up a map at the Office du Tourisme in Ploërmel

And back again at the pretty village of Lizio, you could complete a day by the lake with a visit to the *Ecomusée de la ferme et des métiers* – an exhibition of long-lost trades, their tools and their workshops.

19. A tour of the Île d'Arz

The Île d'Arz is a peaceful green little island at the very heart of the Gulf of Morbihan. This interesting walk follows the coastal footpath and so has a sea-view all the way – and plenty of opportunities for a swim.

Grade: Easy

Distance: 16km (10 miles) in all – but many short cuts are possible

Time: About 4 hours continuous walking, but you will probably want to stop somewhere on the way. Just remember the time of the last boat.

Map: IGN TOP25 0921 OT

Start and Finish: The harbour (Cale de Beluré) at the northernmost tip of the Île d'Arz.

How to get there: An inexpensive ferry service operates 10 times a day in winter and 13 times a day in summer – almost hourly. You can catch the ferry 3 miles south of Vannes at Conleau (from the centre of Vannes, follow signs to 'Le Port' and 'Conleau') or from Barrarac'h (coming from the east, follow signs to the town of Séné, then Port Anna and Barrarac'h). The trip takes about 20 minutes.

Refreshment: There is a hotel/restaurant at the harbour, and a bar/restaurant near the eastern causeway, while the town (le Bourg) has a restaurant, crêperie and a shop. Not all are open in winter.

Notes: This is a very easy walk at all times of the year – walking boots are not a necessity. In summer you should take sun-cream and a hat as much of the walk is quite exposed, and if you enjoy a swim, don't forget your costume – it's an excellent way to cool off on a hot day. If possible, take binoculars with you – the views are magnificent. You may also wish to carry water, although you are never far from access to the town and its facilities. The last boat of the evening is usually quite late – but, be warned, they can be very punctual.

Introduction

Guide books will tell you that the only way to see the Golfe du Morbihan is to take a tour by boat. Here is another suggestion – take a walk around the Île d'Arz and you will see it all, particularly if you remember your binoculars.

The Île d'Arz has the sort of outline you might expect from an ink drop splashed across a page. Fingers of land reach out into the sea giving promontories each with a different view, and between them, curving sandy beaches and tiny coves. Some outlying splashes of land are connected with the main island only by causeways, one of which is backed by an interesting tide-mill. The island is fortunately less popular than its western neighbour the Île aux Moines, where seasonal crowds are attracted by the fine residences and tropical vegetation. The Île d'Arz remains a simpler place of fields, sea and sky, the height of its civilization being the tiny granite town at its centre. In this place you can have a peaceful walk even in the middle of summer. Out of season, although the ferry still runs hourly, you may well have the island pathways entirely to yourself. But do not be deceived, this is not a place without facilities. The bar/restaurant in the little town is open all the year round, as is another restaurant on the island. Where the customers come from on a January day remains a mystery!

This walk is made special by the ever-changing views as you move around the island. The Gulf of Morbihan has proverbially 365 islands – although the number changes with the state of the tide. However many there are, you can see almost all of them from some point around the shores of the Île d'Arz. You can also see the sweep of the Gulf behind from the Rhuys peninsula in the south to Vannes and Arradon in the north. The shallow sea is speckled with boats – sailing boats, fishing vessels, ferries and wind-surfers heading in every direction. But sea views are not all and there are many local points of interest, too.

The coastal path (*Sentier Côtier*) itself is mostly waymarked and easy to follow. One of the advantages of island walking is that it is difficult to get lost! The path is a grassy track hugging the coast almost all the way – only rarely will your feet touch tarmac. The route is mostly open, although at the southern tip are magnificent tall pines that shade the site of a megalith and make a fine picnic spot with a view. Several excellent beaches are passed – being an island, you can always find a sheltered one, whatever the wind's direction. The shallow water on the western side has been dammed to provide power for a tide-mill, while on the east there are old *marais salants* – rectangular pits once used for evaporating and collecting salt from the sea. There is an old manor at Kernoël and a 17th century church in the town. And if, at the end of the tour, you find that island walking has suited you well, there are several possibilities nearby for another day.

The Walk

1. Having left the boat at the slipway (*la Cale*), walk past the hotel/restaurant and continue down the road. Ignore a signpost indicating the *Sentier Côtier* on the left and continue on the road, passing a campsite on the left and skirting a wide sandy beach on the right. (This is the Plage de la Falaise – oddly named, as there isn't a cliff in sight!) Across the water and past some little pine-topped islands, the land you can see is the Île aux Moines, the largest island in the Gulf. It will be in your view for some time as you continue down the western shore. Ahead of you, the Pointe de Berno projects far into the sea, promising fine views when you reach it (in about half an hour)

2. At the end of the beach, the road leaves the shore and heads inland. No waymarks are to be seen, but you should leave the road here beside some conifers before the first houses of the town. Keep beside the shore on a broad grassy track taking you out to a pine-clad promontory ahead. Reaching the tip of this, the

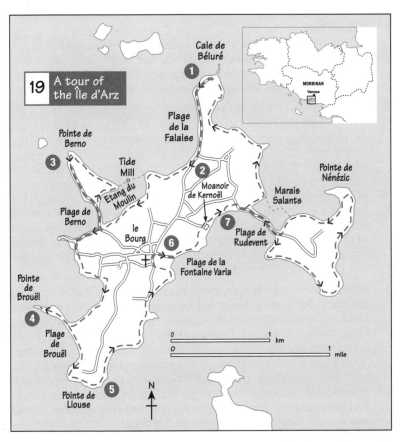

view changes, and in front of you is a low wall cutting off the *Étang du Moulin* – an attractive lake much favoured by wading birds, where skeletons of long-dead boats project from the marsh. On the wall is a tide-mill which is being privately restored, and a notice warns you that you cross the wall at your own risk – the alternative is the path running behind the *étang* and crossing the causeway. Whatever route you take, you are now on a piece of land that is virtually an island and you should continue with the shore on your right to reach the Pointe de Berno. Those little pine-topped islands are just offshore here, and behind them is the Île aux Moines. To the north, other islands are seen (the largest is the Île Drennec, which you passed on the boat as you approached the harbour). Far to the north-west, beyond the Île aux Moines, the Pointe d'Arradon on the mainland reaches out into the sea.

3. Continue now along the western shore, crossing the causeway with the Plage de Berno on your right. Keeping ahead past the little harbour with its slipway, a rocky coastline is reached, and from here, obvious tracks will lead you into town if you wish. Con-

tinuing beside the coast, a *Sentier Côtier* sign directs you to the right to skirt the bay on the way to the Pointe de Brouël ahead. A narrow strip of land finally takes you out to its rocky tip, where now only a narrow channel separates you from the Île aux Moines, and a shrine hides among the gorse bushes.

4. Returning over the causeway, a picnic-table and seats are well-placed for a break in the journey. The Plage de Brouël (now on your right), backed by rocks and pine-trees, is probably the prettiest beach on the island, and is recommended for bathing – and just lying in the sun. Ahead is the southernmost tip of the island, the Pointe de Liouse, a fine viewpoint where the remains of a dolmen are hidden beneath a canopy of tall green firs. From here you are looking south into an arc of large islands – the largest, ahead and to the left, is the Île Ilur – and beyond them is the coast of the Rhuys peninsula near Sarzeau. The southern tip of the Île aux Moines cuts off your view of the end of that peninsula and the exit from the Gulf into the open sea.

5. After the Pointe de Liouse, the path swings around and runs along the cliffs, for a while bordered by tough hedges of thorn as you head north towards the town again. Approaching the little harbour, there is a sailing school and then a pleasant site with picnic tables. Past the slipway, a track to the left beside some tall conifers leads you up into the town. (If you want to give the town a miss, just continue beside the beach). Keeping uphill, you reach the square with its bar/restaurant. Turn right behind the restaurant and keep straight ahead (ignore signs to the *embarcadère* unless you want to return by road to the port, a distance of about 3km) to reach the coastal path again.

6. Bear left, and emerging through a barrier behind some houses, turn left on the track to reach a metalled road. Ahead of you is the old, grey Manoir de Kernoël. Turn left on this road and in about 20 metres, right, into a field. The path skirts the fence of a property to reach a track leading to the sea. Here, turn left between houses to reach a metalled road beside an interesting-looking restaurant proclaiming itself 'Open all Year'. Continue along the road for about 200 metres to a T-junction, and turn right to cross the causeway to the Île de Bilhervé.

7. If you are running short of time or energy, you could omit this part of the walk – the tour around this little island will take you nearly an hour. If you wish to take it, there is a good beach, and a good viewpoint at the Pointe de Bilhervé. Farther on, the path wanders up to the Pointe de Nénézic where a little granite house sits on its own island. The path then follows beside a wide marsh popular with all manner of sea birds at low tide. Returning to cross the causeway again, you have a fine beach on one side of it and on the

A street in le Bourg

other, the *marais salants*. Sea salt was harvested here from the Middle Ages until about a hundred years ago.

Whether or not you have toured the Île de Bilhervé, you are now at the main island end of the causeway (Point 7 on the map). Now follow the *Sentier Côtier* signpost, which takes you out again past marshland at low tide. Your view is across the sea to two low tree-clad islands before the mainland to the north. The path continues round the coast until, just as you think you have reached the harbour, it takes a sharp left turn into a field. The road is soon reached, where turning right will take you back to the harbour.

More Walks in the Area

If this island tour has sparked off a desire to try others, there are several more possibilities :

The Île aux Moines, with more houses, more people and more tropical vegetation than the Île d'Arz, makes a perfectly good day's outing. The path here is not exactly circular, more up and down and sideways, but there are more than 20km of footpaths and some lovely beaches to visit. Catch the ferry from Port-Blanc on the west of the Gulf.

From the end of the Quiberon peninsula there is a boat service to each of three islands out in the sea. The largest of these is Belle-Île-en-Mer, which has a beautiful coastal footpath – the only problem is that it will take you over a week to walk around it. Consider returning for another holiday. The other two, the islands of Houat and Hoëdic, each have a waymarked coastal footpath that can be walked in three or four hours. Hoëdic is the smaller and wilder, with an old fort that is being restored at its centre. Houat is perhaps prettier with fine cliffs, coves and beaches. A day trip to either of these is practical – and different.

There is just one other major island off the coast – the Île de Groix, this time reached by ferry from Lorient. The island again has a waymarked coastal path, which will take about two days to circumnavigate. But smaller circuits are possible, and you can choose between the fine beaches of the south and east and the rocky cliffs of the north and west.

Many more walks are possible elsewhere in the Gulf. The Office du Tourisme in Vannes stocks an inexpensive book of 36 walks in the area – *Randonnées au Pays de Vannes*. Some understanding of French would make things easier, but the maps are good – try the walk at le Hézo on the eastern side of the Gulf. As an alternative, you could start at le Hézo and follow the *Sentier Côtier* (here a Grande Randonnée with white and red waymarks) south via St Armel to Lasné. The path crosses oyster beds in the ancient *marais salants*. An explanation of past and present use is given on the board in the car park beside the sea at Lasné – but again you will need some French. From St Armel you can walk out on a causeway to le Passage (and take a ferry across the estuary in summer), and from Lasné you can walk out to the Île Tascon if the tide is low

Places of interest nearby

The Office du Tourisme in Vannes can provide you with a good map of the area around the Gulf in its free leaflet *Du pays d'Auray à la presqu'il de Rhuys*. They can also find you a town map, which will guide you around the picturesque walled old town area close by. Attractive traditional houses, ancient ramparts, old lavoirs, a covered medieval market, and the cathedral with its cloisters and fine formal gardens all contribute to a most interesting morning's stroll.

Venturing again into the Gulf, the island of Gavrinis near its sea entrance is well worth a visit. This tiny island is home to perhaps the most remarkable megalithic site in Brittany, a tumulus so large that it is the highest point in the Gulf and can be seen from the sea as you cross. Beneath a grass-topped stone cairn, a long corridor, its supports decorated with ancient carvings, leads on to a burial chamber dating from about 4000BC. Boats cross frequently (in summer only) from Larmor Baden on the west coast.

And if you want more megaliths, surely another contender for the most remarkable site is Carnac, on the coast just west of the Gulf. To the north of the town is an amazing collection of alignments in various sites – the ones at Kermario have nearly a thousand stones in ten rows. The whole area is scattered with menhirs, tumuli and dolmens and is a must if you are anywhere in range.

Fountain, seat and cross near Ménez-Hom

Finistère

20. The enchanted forest of Huelgoat

In the ancient woodland beside the town of Huelgoat, the valley of the River Argent holds an amazing assortment of caves, pools, waterfalls and rock formations. For added measure, this walk follows an old canal to reach a silver mine deep in the forest and climbs to a Celtic hill fort with magnificent views.

Grade: Moderate

Distance: 14km (8¾ miles) – but two short cuts are possible, cutting out a total of 5km

Time: 4 hours for whole route.

Map: IGN Série Bleue 0617 E

Start and finish: Lakeside car park at Huelgoat

How to get there: Huelgoat lies just off the D764, 35km south of Morlaix (and 15km north of Carhaix-Plouguer). The lake is on the eastern side of the town and easy to find – just follow the signs. There are parking spaces all along the promenade – but if you have difficulty, there are other car parks in the town.

Refreshment: There is a good variety of restaurants, bars and cafés in Huelgoat. En route, there is a crêperie near the Maré aux Sangliers (between points 4 and 5 on the map)

Notes: This walk is quite suitable for trainers in dry weather in summer – at other times, walking boots are preferable. If you intend to do the whole walk, it might be a good idea to carry fluid – there is only one place where you can get refreshment on the way. Since most of the route is in the forest, there is good shade on a hot day – although the climb to Arthur's Camp is exposed. And if you find the distance too great, you can easily opt for a short cut.

Waymarking: The route is waymarked in yellow throughout.

Introduction

This has to be inland Brittany's top walk – the only possible drawback is that in summer you may find you have rather more friends than you had bargained for to share your path! But whatever the season you should not miss the opportunity to visit this fine ancient forest which is part of the Armorique National Park.

Before the arrival of the Romans, all central Brittany was covered with forest such as this – now only Huelgoat and a handful of other places remain. It is a forest of oak and beech, here covering granite slopes and deep valleys where rocks have been eroded over thousands of years to produce weird shapes and strange formations. These are the 'sites', and each has been given an imaginative – if rather fanciful – name. The Grotte du Diable, Théâtre de Verdure, Roche Tremblante and Ménage de la Vierge (where the rocks are supposed to look like cooking utensils) are all within easy reach of the town.

The River Argent

Farther afield there are more named sites, some beautiful, some spectacular. Le Gouffre is a chasm where the river disappears into an underground waterfall and below it is the Maré aux Fées – a delightful fairy pool. Farther on is the Maré aux Sangliers (Wild Boar Pool – yes, there are those in the forest!) and the Arthurian legends, too, make their appearance with the Grotte d'Artus and Camp d'Artus.

The walk visits all these sites, but first sets out along the bank of a narrow canal that winds its way through the woodland for some 3km. It is one of two canals that were constructed in the 18th century to service a lead and silver mine – a mine previously known to the Romans. The canal water not only washed the ore but also provided power for the engines. The path beside the canal is very attractive (try it in Autumn colours), but there is so much to see later on this walk you may want to take advantage of a short cut that halves the distance. Arriving at the mine, you can still see its entrances and various old buildings – a display board points out the features.

Beyond the mine the route takes an incredibly beautiful path beside the River Argent, passing the pretty Maré aux Fées and climbing to the spectacular Gouffre. Further on, a delightful horse-shoe path (Fer à Cheval) takes you high above the river before you continue climbing past the Maré aux Sangliers to the Cave and Camp of Arthur. Despite these legendary connections, the excavations of Sir Mortimer Wheeler in the 1930s proved it to be the site of a Gaulish camp, later taken over by the Romans to house their legions. There are commanding views of the surrounding countryside.

Returning to the rocky valley of the Argent, it is time to test the 100-tonne Roche Tremblante. Apparently it rocks gently when given just a slight push – but you have to find the right spot to apply the pressure. At least no-one seems to have pushed too hard as yet! And just before you emerge in the town you can make a descent into the Grotte du Diable on an iron ladder. The story is that a revolutionary soldier, pursued by the Chouans (the Breton anti-revolutionaries), hid in this cave and lit a fire to keep himself warm. The pursuing army, seeing a man with a pitchfork in a red glow, thought they had come across the devil himself!

The walk reaches the town beside the Moulin du Chaos, an old mill above a waterfall and rocky gorge with huge boulders in its bed. The mill now houses the Office du Tourisme – where you might like to call and find out about more walks in this magical forest.

The Walk

1. Leave the lakeside promenade by the main road at its centre, the Rue du Général de Gaulle. This passes the town square on the left and becomes the Rue Docteur Jacq. Continue on this road to the edge of the town. After a very sharp left-hand bend, signs for *Promenade du Canal* and *Site de la Mine* point you off on the right to join the canalside path. The path now keeps to the left bank of the narrow canal as it winds and twists its way through beautiful woodland around the sides of the valley. The constant changes of direction leave you quite bemused until suddenly you come upon the little building of the hydro-electric station.

2. From this point you can choose to take a short cut to reach the mine (follow 2a) or continue along the canal path to reach the same point in a further 2km(2b)

2a. Crossing the bridge and walking around the back of the electricity building, take the path on the left – you will find a yellow flash on a tree showing you the way. This path heads straight downhill, crosses a little clearing, and soon crosses the bed of the older second canal. Now bear right following the yellow arrow on the tree and gain a wider downhill path, which emerges from the woods on a bare plateau. Bear right to cross the river on a little log bridge and reach the display board and buildings of the mine.

2b To take the canalside path from the electricity station, cross the metal bridge and bear right following the yellow flashed signs to *L'Ancienne Mine*. The canal now is out of water, but you continue beside its bed to the head of the valley, where the entrant stream is crossed on a little bridge. A further 15 minutes walk brings you to the top of the mine beside a gallery entrance. Continue ahead to the broad stony road and turn left heading downhill following the yellow flashes. At the junction, again bear left, heading for the

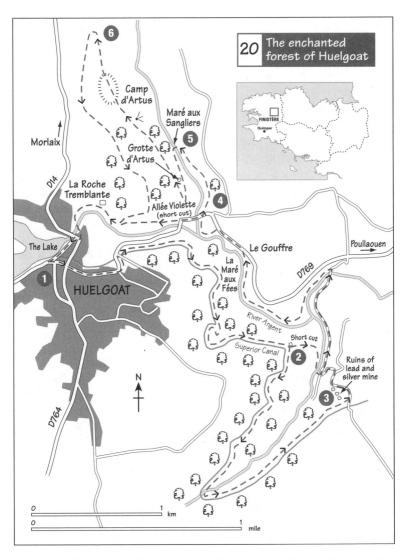

lower buildings of the mine. At the bottom of the hill, the mine entrance is on the left beyond the display board.

3. When you have had enough of the mine, leave it along the broad stony access road with the river on your left and continue to the bridge. The waymarks indicate that you have joined the route of a Grande Randonnée (white on red). On the far side of the bridge is a wooden signpost where you turn left and follow the direction of the GR 37 to Huelgoat. The path climbs into the woods and soon follows the banks of a river to reach the Maré aux Fees. Climbing more steeply beside the tumbling river, you arrive at the Gouffre, where the river falls through 8 metres and disappears under blocks of granite. Steps lead you up to the road, and you have the option of climbing to the *Belvédère*, a viewpoint high on the rock. Now turn left on the road, and in about 200 metres, take the path on the left marked *Fer à Cheval*. This very pretty path is a worthwhile alternative to the sharp corner on the road.

4. When you reach the road again you have a choice. If you wish to return by the quickest route to the starting point (approx. 1km), follow 4a. To continue with the main walk, follow 4b.

4a Turn left on the road and continue for 100 metres to the Pont-Rouge, just after the sharp corner. Just before this bridge, the most attractive Allée Violette continues into the woods on the right of the river. About 300 metres along, the Stèle des Fusillés high on the bank on the right marks the place of execution of resistance fighters in 1944. At the end of this path you pass the Ménage de la Vierge (real evidence of a fertile imagination here!) and bear right to reach La Roche Tremblante. From here you should be able to follow the yellow flashes to visit the other sites and return to the lake – but if you have difficulties, see Point 6.

4b Cross the road diagonally to the right to the car parking area beside the river. From here take the Sentier du Clair Ruisseau, a path that climbs above the river. After about 400 metres, a sign points to a crêperie on the right (this may be very welcome by now!). Almost immediately, another sign directs you left to the Maré aux Sangliers. At the bottom of the steps is a little pool with huge rounded boulders and a wooden bridge crossing the water. One boulder is topped by a tree-stump and encircled by its roots – a sad reminder of the storm of October 1987 when this proud pine like so many others in the forest was brought to the ground. Continuing over the pool, you climb to a metalled road.

5. Turn left on this road and pass the cave called Grotte d'Artus. Soon afterwards, a road on the right is signed to the Camp d'Artus. Continue on this road following the yellow waymarks, and passing on your left the Sentier des Amoureux. The road climbs quite steeply and there are viewpoints on the right before you enter the camp between two huge granite boulders. The Roman walls of the camp are quite obvious and on the far side a display board describes its features.

6. Continuing downhill to the barrier, you turn left following the yellow waymarks on the Sentier du Louarn. This picturesque path winds through gorse and bracken and round rocks on the side of the hill. After about 10 minutes of this, you come to a path cross-roads. The waymarks, which have been excellent until now, are unaccountably absent. Turn right, downhill, at this junction,

heading for La Roche Tremblante, after a while again picking up the yellow flashes. At a fork with a waymarked rock, keep left and continue downhill beside a low wall to reach a stream.

Now bear up to the right to the huge rock on the hill – La Roche Tremblante at last! When you have satisfied yourself that you can't move it (can anyone?) continue up the stone steps in the rock behind and follow the yellow flashes to the left, and then to the left downhill beside a rock-face with a big cave. Opposite you across the river is the Théâtre de Verdure and if you turned left on the riverside path you would reach the Ménage de la Vierge. But to continue, cross over the chaos of rocks in the riverbed and bear right to reach the Grotte du Diable. From here, the flashes lead you through a rocky passage to emerge beside the Moulin du Chaos, the very last of the forest 'sites' – at least, on this walk.

Other Walks in the Area

The Office du Tourisme in the Moulin du Chaos stocks a fine assortment of literature on the forest and surrounding area. There are various free leaflets, and another very inexpensive one, *Promenades Pédestres et Circuits en boucle de Petites Randonnées*. The latter maps out the circuits within a radius of 2km and also circuits farther afield, said to be within 4km. The yellow one of these is the route you have just completed, but each of the other four is interesting in its own right and waymarked in colour in a similar fashion to this one. Both green and blue routes visit the Menhir de Kerampeulven, a splendid tall standing stone noted for its engravings of animals. Although these are undoubtedly old, they most certainly post-date the menhir itself. Of the short walks possible from Huelgoat, it is certainly worth visiting the viewpoint called La Roche Cintrée. From here you can see across to the Monts d'Arrée in the north-west – a view that may well tempt you to try Walk 24.

Two waymarked circuits in the forest start from Locmaria-Berrien, 6km to the east. A very pretty and largely forested route is the *Circuit des Deux Vallées* (10km), which follows the River Argent on its way to join the Aulne. A rather longer waymarked route (14km) starts from the old silver mine and passes through several pretty hamlets before returning along the route of the old Roman road between Morlaix and Carhaix. Details of both these walks are in the free leaflet *Locmaria-Berrien Randonnée*, which again you can find at the Office du Tourisme in Huelgoat.

Places of interest nearby

Huelgoat is on the eastern edge of the Armorique Natural Regional Park. This rather odd-shaped park stretches out in a narrow band westwards from Huelgoat to reach the tip of the Crozon peninsula – and even beyond to the islands of Molène and Ouessant. Included in this area are the Monts d'Arrée, just west of Huelgoat, the highest 'mountains' in Brittany. From the Roc'h Trévezel (384m) on a fine day you can see all north-west Brittany – from Lannion Bay in the north to Brest in the west and to the Montagnes Noires in the South. There are also fine views from the Mont St Michel de Brasparts (Ménez Mikel in Breton) – see Walk 24. This mountain overlooks the eerie peat-bog of Yeun Elez and the dark reservoir of St Michel – unfortunately the wild landscape is not improved by the presence of a nuclear power station.

Apart from its wild scenery, the region of the Monts d'Arrée is also known for its parish closes (*les enclos paroissiaux*), which though found all over Brittany, are at their most elaborate here (said to be due to inter-village rivalry). The enclosed combination of church, ossuary, calvary and cemetery gave scope for some of the most intricate and detailed stonework and carvings, mostly dating from around the 16th century, and contrasting starkly with the poverty of village life at the time. The best examples are at St Thégonnec, Guimiliau and Lampaul-Guimiliau, approximately 35km north-west of Huelgoat – and there is even a 'Parish Close Trail' if you become interested.

If parish closes are not to your taste, the Monts d'Arrée offer you also a wealth of eco – museums – flora, fauna, geology, water-mills, farming, craftsmanship and every other aspect of local life seems to have its own little exhibition centre – just ask at the Office du Tourisme.

21. With the Painters of Pont-Aven

For over 150 years, the colourful little town of Pont-Aven has attracted artists from all over the world – the most famous of them all, Paul Gauguin. On this walk there is the excitement of visiting the scenes that inspired some of his paintings, followed by a return along the wooded banks of the winding River Aven, one of the prettiest rivers in Brittany

Grade: Easy

Distance: 11km (7 miles) with shorter 8km option

Time: 3 hours (shorter walk about 2 hours)

Map: IGN Top 25 0620 ET

Start and finish: The port at Pont-Aven

How to get there: Pont-Aven is at the head of an estuary on the south coast, mid-way between Quimper and Lorient. From the main bridge in the town, follow the road along the west bank of the river to the port (well-sign-posted), where there is plenty of parking – but, be warned, Pont-Aven is very popular and parking spaces may be at a premium at the height of the season. There are other sign-posted car-parks further away from the town centre.

Refreshment: There are many bars and eating houses of all kinds in Pont-Aven. It is also possible to get refreshment en route at the little village of Nizon.

Notes: This is a very easy walk, quite suitable for trainers in summertime. Even out of season there should not be much problem, but you may appreciate a pair of boots on the woodland sections which can be a little muddy. After Nizon you can choose to return directly to Pont-Aven, although the longer walk including the picturesque banks of the estuary is highly recommended.

Waymarking: The path through the Bois d'Amour is waymarked in yellow. There is no further waymarking until you reach Point 8, after which you follow the white on red marks of the Grande Randonneée.

Introduction

It was in 1886 that Paul Gauguin arrived in Pont-Aven. Artists had been there before him and artists are still there today, but his brief stay of three years was enough to ensure a place in history – and a never-ending stream of visitors – for this little fishing port. For here, in Pont-Aven, Gauguin and his friend Émile Bernard evolved their new and entirely original form of painting now known as synthetism – a style that rejected conventional perspective, where vivid blocks of strong colour were surrounded by thick and heavy lines. It was a style as suited to the landscapes and religious themes of Brittany as it was later to be to the islands of the South Seas

Gauguin and his colleagues lived near the bridge, in a lodging house that is now a newsagents shop – look for the plaque on the wall.

The harbour at Pont-Aven

You can still appreciate the scene that drew them here. Pont-Aven was a town of fourteen water-mills – most of them are still around in various states of repair, gracing the banks of the rushing, tumbling, rock-strewn river. Almost magically, that river opens into a wide calm estuary and an attractive port, which in Gauguin's time busied itself with transhipment of corn for the mills. Now, pleasure craft alone use the port but the prospect is still a pleasing one. Below the port, woods crowd to the water's edge along both sides of the estuary, and the path home is delightful.

There are more woods at the start of the walk. The Bois d'Amour, most attractive beech woods beside the river above the town, provide your first encounter with the Pont-Aven school of synthetists. Gauguin here taught his pupil Paul Sérusier, and the painting which was produced that day – on the lid of a cigar box! – has become famous as *The Talisman*. The little house you pass in the woods is the *Moulin Neuf* seen in that painting. Climbing out of the trees to the hill above, you next come upon Gauguin at the strange, lop-sided, grey stone Chapelle de Trémalo. Inside is a 17th century yellow wooden calvary, which was the inspiration for his *Christ Jaune*, a painting now, like so many others, housed across the Atlantic. Sunken tree-lined lanes lead you on to the village of Nizon where another calvary, now a classically Breton one outside in the square, provided the inspiration for Gauguin's *Christ Vert*. But if you want to see more recent crafts-manship, try to get inside the church here. The stained glass windows by Guével are truly of the most glorious colours and well worth a pause on your journey.

After Nizon, the route passes the obviously haunted ruins of the 15th century Château de Rustéphan, concealed in the woods. It, too, was the subject of a painting, this time by Émile Bernard. Artists are then left behind as you head for the estuary to follow the Grande Randonnée along its shores. Meandering along the rocky, tree-lined banks with views of boats and water, just this short stretch of path is guaranteed to lure you back to the GR 34 – another day!

The Walk

1. Walk from the port towards the bridge in the centre of the town. On the way you can see water-mills on both sides of the river, one of them converted into a first-class restaurant. Do not cross the bridge, but continue ahead up the Rue Émile Bernard – note the little Gothic-style loo on the river bank. Take the first turning on the right – the Promenade Xavier Graal. This flower-bedecked path on an island in the river is dedicated to a native poet and journalist. Once over the footbridge to the island, turn left, but soon turn left again, crossing another footbridge to leave the island and reach a road. Now turn right and continue uphill on the road almost to the top, where a sign on the right points to the Bois d'Amour. Following the sign, you will cross under the bridge to emerge in splendid beech woods with rocks cascading to the river.

2. Keep to the broad path beside the river for about 800 metres, passing on the way a small grey stone cottage which was the 'Moulin Neuf' of the *Talisman* painting. On reaching the tarmacked road, turn left towards the trout farm and, almost immediately, left again up the hill on a track once more in the woods. Near the top of the hill is a clear junction, where you now leave the Bois d'Amour circuit, and turn right along a track lined by tall trees. After about 200 metres, you arrive at the gates of the Château du Pléssis.

3. Here turn left between an avenue of trees that ends at the farm of Quistilliou. At this farm, the road bends left, and following it around, you come to a junction at a corner where the road takes a sharp left-hand bend. From here take the lane that goes straight ahead to reach the Chapelle de Trémalo. The little chapel is usually open and you can admire the old beams and carvings of the interior as well as the calvary that was the model for Gauguin's painting.

4. Just past the chapel, take the tree-lined track to the right sign-posted to Ste. Maude. This bears left at the top into another broad track beside woods. Soon a small road crosses the track and

you keep straight ahead into a shady alley between earth banks. Another road crosses and again you keep ahead on a sunken track. After passing a farm on the left you reach the D24. Here turn right and in about 30 metres, left on a metalled road that leads into Nizon. Passing a lavoir – a village washing place, which in this case is still in use – you arrive at a car park in a square. Now double back to the right on a small road that climbs behind some fine old oak trees, and at the T-junction, turn left to reach the church with its ornate calvary that was Gauguin's inspiration. If the church is locked, it should be possible to obtain the key – those windows are magnificent from the inside only.

5. If you are walking at the height of summer, it is possible that you have not exactly been alone on the route so far. But now it is time to leave Gauguin and his many admirers and head off towards the estuary. Leave the church on the Rue des Grands Chênes and again reach the car park in the square. Keep this on your left and continue ahead for about 400 metres to a cross-roads. Now turn right, and after just about the same distance, turn right again, sign-posted to Rustéphan. Just before the farm buildings, take the track into the woods on the left. The ivy-clad remains of the Château de Rustéphan peer eerily through the trees on your right. Continue ahead on the woodland track and you will soon find yourself walking beside an old wall between trees that once lined the drive to the château. On reaching the tarmacked road, turn right for 20 metres to reach the main D783.

6. On the opposite side of the D783 is a lay-by with picnic tables and toilets. Cross straight over to take the road opposite, which leaves through the lay-by (S.P. Kernonen). Keep on this road for about 800 metres, then at a cross-roads, turn left on a quiet pleasant road beside and through woodland. After about 500 metres, a larger road is reached and you have a choice. To return directly to Pont-Aven, go now to the SHORT CUT instructions, which are printed at the end of the main walk text.

7. To continue with the main walk, turn right here and walk along the grassy verge beside the road for about 800 metres to a road junction in the village of Kerrun. On the way, after a left-hand bend, look right to see a huge menhir beside the road. At the junction, bear left, and at the next junction (20 metres), keep straight ahead (ignore signs to Kerrun here). Continuing downhill for about 300 metres, just after the road bends right, you will see a stone arch on the left where a broad track leaves the road.

8. Turn left here (S.P. Kerscaff Tal-Moor) and follow the gravelly track with stream on the right to reach a fork. Ignore the white on red Grande Randonnée waymarks to the right and keep to the left

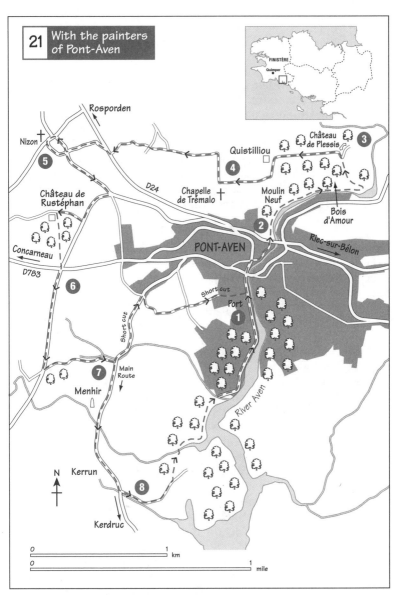

21 With the painters of Pont-Aven

FINISTÈRE
Quimper

Rosporden

Nizon

Château de Plessis

Quistilliou

3

5

4

D24

Chapelle de Trémalo

Moulin Neuf

Château de Rustéphan

Bois d'Amour

Concarneau

2

PONT-AVEN

Riec-sur-Bélon

D783

6

Short cut

Port

1

Short cut

7

Main Route

River Aven

Menhir

N

Kerrun

8

Kerdruc

0   1
          km
0   1
                     mile

here, away from the houses. In about 150 metres, at a junction with a stone wall ahead, bear left following some more GR waymarks on a tree. The path goes through an alley between the trees, at the bottom of which you cross over a wall and continue on a path through the woods. After a while (and some stone steps) you will pick up a Sentier Côtier sign and more GR marks. The way back is now easy to follow, a most attractive path winding through the trees beside the estuary. All too soon you will reach a car park, and from there you continue on the little road beside the estuary, still with fine views, to reach the port at Pont-Aven.

Short Cut

At Point 7, turn left on the road, and follow it for about 800 metres. At a cross-roads in a village, turn right on a grassy and stony track running past houses for about 400 metres. At the tar-macked road, cross straight over and go ahead down another rough road. At its end, a grey stone wall faces you and there are tracks left, right and centre. Take the grassy track ahead and follow it downhill as it bends and winds, goes down steps and finally emerges on a tarmacked road which comes out on the promenade near the bridge. Turn right to reach the port.

More Walks in the Area

The well-waymarked GR34 follows the attractive west bank of the Aven to reach the sea at Port Manec'h – a distance of about 13km, which will take you about 3½ hours. Tourist Information at Pont-Aven has a good map on the back of its free leaflet *Au fil de l'Aven et du Belon*. Unfortunately there is no bus service, so you will need a taxi to return.

For a shorter walk, you could park in the woodland car park just past the sea mill at Hénant and follow the Grande Randonnée along the west bank as far as Kerdruc (4km), a most picturesque little port with a couple of bar/restaurants to provide you with lunch. Return in the afternoon or get someone to pick you up.

Farther afield, the GR34 follows the coast to the west and east of the Aven estuary. To the west are cliffs and fine beaches, including Raguénez Plage with its island, while to the east, beyond the estuary of the Bélon, the coast is more rugged with cliffs, coves and fishing villages. The route is clearly shown on the IGN map mentioned above, and the waymarking on the ground is first-class.

The Office du Tourisme, in the main square at Pont-Aven, has information on various circular routes. If you invest a few francs in the pocket-sized folder *Guide de Balades au Pays des Portes de Cornouaille*, you will have a map showing all the waymarked walks and cycle rides in the area – and there are many! On the accompanying folders, the routes are drawn out in more detail. There is no text to the walks, just a few words to tell you the points of interest in each. The waymarking for these routes is excellent – you should have no trouble getting around any one of them – take your choice.

Places of interest nearby

Pont-Aven itself is full of interest – although it unfortunately may be rather crowded in summer. Artists' galleries and exhibitions are everywhere, and the town's *Musée* is worth a visit. There are plenty of paintings from the Pont-Aven school, but disappointingly, Gauguin himself is represented by only a couple of canvasses which do not seem to bear much relation to the splendours of his work to come.

Going farther away, the little ports of Kerdruc and Port Manec'h on the estuary of the Aven are each delightful – they are mentioned in the Other Walks section. Farther east, the tiny port of Brigneau on its own estuary is an interesting place, and here you can see a few of the old thatched cottages (chaumières)

Kerascoët and Kercanic, two villages to the south-west of Pont-Aven, are well preserved as *villages typiques*. Here again are the thatched houses, but (particularly in Kerascoët) you can see the *pierres debout* – huge granite stones more than 2m. high – of which the houses of three or four hundred years ago were constructed.

If you have worked up an interest in Gauguin, you could pursue him to the seaside town of le Pouldu (south-east), to which he retreated after Pont-Aven. Here he lived at an inn that is now the Café de la Plage and achieved notoriety by swimming naked in the sea. As usual, he was penniless and left le Pouldu for the South Seas after paying his landlady with only few paintings that he left behind. These, of course, are now priceless and no longer in le Pouldu – but you can see prints of them at the well-reconstructed *Maison Marie Henry*.

22. Coastal scenes at Carantec

The pretty resort of Carantec overlooks a scattering of islands in the Bay of Morlaix. This is a coastal walk for all the family, passing a succession of beaches and viewpoints, with the opportunity to visit the Île Callot, an island only accessible by causeway at low tide.

Grade: Easy

Distance: 10km (6¼ miles) The optional walk from the port to the end of the Île Callot is a further 3km each way – note it is only possible at low water! At this time, it is also possible to take a car across the causeway to one of the designated parking areas and continue on foot to the end.

Time: About 2½ hours walking – but you may wish to stop at the beaches or for refreshment.

Map: IGN TOP 25 0615 ET, but the Office du Tourisme can provide you with a simple free map that covers it all.

Start and finish: The port at Carantec – the start of the causeway to the Île Callot.

How to get there: From Morlaix take the D73 – this is the coastal road, and much prettier than the much faster D58 you are encouraged to use. Arriving in Carantec, head for the centre of the town and then follow signs for *le port* and *Île Callot*. There is some parking alongside the port and another car park a short distance away.

Refreshment: Carantec has lots of restaurants – a list of them is given on the free map. Walking through the town, you will pass a bar/restaurant, and there are three restaurants together, all with inside and outside seating, at the Plage du Kelenn. There are more bars and restaurants at the port. There is no refreshment on the Île Callot.

Notes: This is an easy walk with no footwear requirements other than a pair of trainers. The route follows the coastal path, which although sometimes narrow, is in no way dangerous. There are a few gentle climbs and descents. The short section through the town is on roads. If the weather is hot, think of sun-screen – and don't forget your bathing costume as the route actually crosses the two best beaches. Two more additions to your rucksack might be water and binoculars. And if you want to go out to the Île Callot, check the hours of the tides, which are posted at the end of the causeway.

Waymarking: The *Sentier Côtier* here is the GR 34 – and so bears the white on red waymarks of a Grande Randonnée. The section through the town is not waymarked.

Introduction

Carantec has an enviable position on a hilly peninsula breaking into the heart of the Bay of Morlaix. Once the place was nothing more than a little fishing village, but a century or so ago, Parisians spotted its potential as a resort and things began to change. Hotels were built,

Restaurants on the Plage du Kélenn, Carantec

and Carantec became 'fashionable' – but happily it remained unspoilt and is today a favourite destination for family holidays. Sandy beaches are on all sides, and the views in the bay are in the best traditions of Brittany – cliffs, coves, boats, pines and a myriad of rocky islands in a turquoise sea. The walk here will take you all around the peninsula, passing many of those beaches and a further variety of viewpoints, each with its own aspect on the bay. An optional addition is the walk out to the Île Callot, which will need to be timed according to the tide.

On the peninsula's western shores where the walk begins, the views are across the estuary of the Penzé to the slender spires of the cathedral and the bell tower of the Kreisker Chapel at St Pol-de-Léon. Beyond is the port of Roscoff, usually dominated by the vast bulk of the currently docked member of the Brittany Ferries fleet. The route from here crosses the town to the eastern shore, where the views are of the Rade de Morlaix, the estuary of the Morlaix River before it empties into the bay. Farther on you reach the Pointe de Pen al Lann and its viewpoint over some interesting offshore islands. The nearer is the green Île Louët with its little lighthouse, while on the island behind, the grey bulk of the Château du Taureau seems to rise directly from the sea. The fortress you see today is unmistakably the work of Vauban, but it was built on the site of an earlier defence created here by the people of Morlaix after an English raid in 1522. Morlaix was sacked while its dignitaries were out feasting and they vowed that never again would the town be taken unawares. In recent years the fort has found use as a prison, as a private residence, and as a sailing school.

From Pen al Lann the walk continues on the northern shore, where the Pointe de Cosmeur and the Chaise du Curé give views over the more distant islands in the bay, which are now an ornithological reserve. One fine beach succeeds another here, and you may well feel tempted to stop at the attractive informal restaurants of the Plage du Kélenn before returning to the port.

Either before or after your walk, a visit to the Île Callot is a must, if only for the adventure of crossing the causeway. The island has its history: in the 6th century it was a base for marauding Danes, pirates who stashed their ill-gotten gains out here. The local Breton ruler was Christian, and he vowed to Our Lady that if he could vanquish the Danes he would build a chapel dedicated to her on the site where the chief Dane had pitched his tent. All went according to plan, and the attractive chapel of Notre Dame de Toute Puissance (Our Lady of all Power) is today a place of pilgrimage. Around the chapel is a village with a farm and typically Breton fields of artichokes. Farther out, the tip of the island is a nature reserve with splendid wild flowers and more excellent views – a pleasant spot to picnic and watch birds and boats going about their business. But don't forget the hour of the tide!

The Walk

1.   From the end of the causeway, walk along the Rue du Port (with the sea on your right). At its end, the road turns away left, but you go down on to the beach, following the white on red waymarks of the Grande Randonnée. Continue along the shore for some 20 minutes, passing the Sibiril monument to sea and finally crossing in front of the Sibiril boatyards. Ernest Sibiril was a wartime Resistance fighter, and with his colleague M. Guegen, was responsible for a network which allowed almost two hundred allies to escape from occupied France. Having crossed over the slipways on the shore, look for a narrow alley on the left, alongside the wall immediately before the oyster farm.

2.   This short alley leads to a road, which you cross directly to the stony track opposite. Now climb uphill, with increasingly fine views behind you across the bay. At the fork, keep right and the track soon becomes a tarmacked road leading to a T-junction. At this junction turn left to reach the roundabout, where you go straight ahead following the signs to *Centre Ville*. At the second roundabout in about 200 metres, again follow the *Centre Ville* signs, this time bearing right. A further 300 metres walking brings you to a third roundabout with a bar/restaurant on the corner. Go straight ahead on the Rue François de Kergrist, a pleasant small road with some attractive residences.

3.   At the end of this road, turn right on the Rue de Tourville, following signs to the Plage de Kélenn. Keep ahead on this road for about 400 metres (ignoring signs to the Plage de Clouët) to yet another roundabout. Here keep straight ahead following signs to the

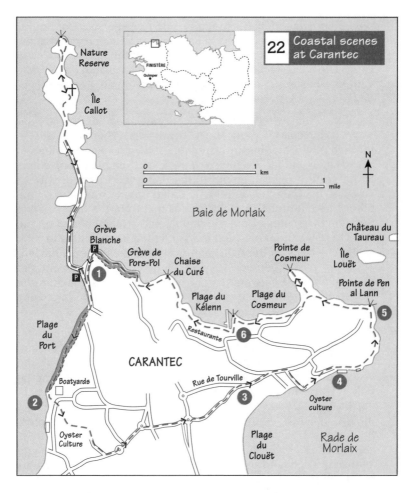

Pointe de Cosmeur, and again pick up the waymarks of the Grande Randonnée. After about 100 metres, these direct you to turn right into a little road heading downhill to the sea again. There are fine views of the long sandy Plage du Clouët and across the estuary of the Morlaix River to the Point de Barnenez.

4. At the oyster culture centre, keep straight ahead between the buildings. If you have the feeling you are in a place where you are unwelcome, you will soon be reassured. At the end of the line is the *Maison de Huitres*, where the proprietor will be only too pleased to sell you some for supper. Continue now behind the building, ignoring the broad uphill track. Soon the waymarks invite you to step on to the beach again – but almost immediately direct you to leave it, turning up some steps into the shade of tall pine trees. This is the Parc Claude Goudo, the sheltered climate of the bay proving ideal for its exotic and rare species. Continuing ahead, the views change again and there is a fine prospect of the Château du Taureau and the Île Louët from the Pointe de Pen al Lann. The white-faced wall is a daymark, intended to be lined up with another at sea, thereby guiding small boats through these dangerous rock-strewn waters.

5. From the Pointe de Pen al Lann, continue ahead on the obvious waymarked coastal path above the beach. The track weaves through pines, dipping and climbing, still with splendid views of islands near and far. Coming to a track junction, you keep ahead and then turn right to go out to the Pointe de Cosmeur with its views across Carantec and the Île Callot on one side, and on the other, the multitude of rocky islands that form the bird reserve. Retracing your steps from the point, keep straight ahead on the track to reach the tarmacked road and then immediately leave it again on a track on the right, sign-posted to the Plage du Kélenn. This track passes behind the wide, sandy Plage du Cosmeur and then climbs to a viewpoint from which you can see across the golden Plage du Kélenn with its sailing school and welcoming array of restaurants.

6. From the viewpoint, descend to the beach passing a picnic site. Cross the beach itself to a path that climbs steeply on the far side. Following the waymarks, you soon arrive at a final viewpoint, the Chaise du Curé, from which you can view the length of the Île Callot with its little chapel. The path goes on downhill, and reaching the tarmac, you turn right to go down to the beach again. Cross the first beach, keep to the right around the stone wall, and cross the second fine sandy beach to an alley on the far side. The waymarks bring you out to a parking area from which you can keep to the right and again go down to the beach to reach the start of the causeway to the Île Callot.

The Walk to the Île Callot

Crossing the causeway, there is only one road on the island, off which are two parking places. From these, the road continues into the village, and then becomes a track to the end of the island, with a circular loop through the nature reserve. It is impossible to get lost – but not to miss the tide, so take care.

More Walks in the Area

From Carantec, the GR 34 continues south beside the estuary, where Morlaix is reached after about 20km – a day's walk. The route is spectacular all the way, particularly at its southern end where the path winds through woods above the river. A bus service operates between Carantec and Morlaix – either Office du Tourisme can give you times, or help you instead to find a taxi. The waymarking of the GR is excellent, but it would probably help to acquire the Top 25 map mentioned earlier.

Beyond Morlaix, the Grande Randonnée climbs to yet another peninsula, that of Barnenez. Around this there is a fine short circular walk of about 4km, a route which circles the 6000-year-old Cairn de Barnenez, one of the most impressive of Brittany's megalithic sites (see the Places of Interest section below). The short route can be extended by taking a further circuit up the coast to Térénez. Both this routes and its extension are waymarked and can be found in the Topoguide *Morlaix, Trégor, Monts d'Arrée (Ref. 056)*. They can also be followed using the aforementioned Top 25 map, on which the paths are clearly marked in red.

The Topoguide *Morlaix, Trégor, Monts d'Arrée* can offer you an interesting choice of walks in the area – although it is, of course, published only in French. However, all the walks it contains are well-waymarked. For something inland, consider the walk up the wooded valley of the River Dourduff starting from the pretty port of Le Dourduff-en-Mer – a circuit of about 14km The route from St Jean-du-Doigt is longer and rather more strenuous – but the coastal path is spectacular. Both these walks again can be followed from the IGN Top 25 map 0615 ET as an alternative to the Topoguide.

Places of interest nearby

The Cairn de Barnenez, mentioned in the More Walks section, is barely 2km from Carantec 'as the crow flies'. But you will have to drive inland past Morlaix to reach it. This huge tumulus, a pile of stones 90 metres long and 7 metres high, was built over 6,000 years ago, on a bare slope overlooking the attractive bay. Unfortunately, the enthusiastic road builders of the 20th century discovered it, and much stone was taken away. A further 12 years was needed to restore it, but this has been well done, and the site is now protected. There is an entrance fee and exhibition.

In high season, you can take a cruise around the bay and up the Morlaix River, or across to the Île de Batz. The Office du Tourisme can give you details. The Île de Batz should perhaps be included in the More Walks section – there is a fine coastal path, about 10km in length, circling the island. Bikes can be hired, you can climb the lighthouse and visit the exotic garden – and the church contains a piece of cloth from the 8th century said to be part of a stole in which St Paul the Aurelian caught the local terrorising dragon!

Roscoff itself is worth a visit – it has far more to offer than its Brittany Ferries terminal. The seaweed industry is prominent here, and there are two establishments where you can find out all about it, taste it and apply it to your skin in various guises. Discovery walks along the shore are also on offer. Again in Roscoff, you can visit the aquarium and the tropical garden – and if you want to see the living contents of your seafood platter, go down to the seawater basins at Les Viviers.

23. Rough seas off Porspoder

The far north-west of Finistère is the region of the Abers, where, between broad estuaries, long granite fingers of land reach out into the wild Atlantic. This walk follows that ragged coastline, and returns past one of the tallest menhirs in Brittany.

Grade: Easy

Distance: 11km (7 miles)

Time: 3 hours

Map: IGN TOP 25 0416 ET

Start and finish: The church at Porspoder

How to get there: From Ploudalmézeau, take the D168 to Kersaint, and then the D27 south-west to Porspoder. The houses of the town stretch for over a kilometre along this road, with the church about in the middle, on the right-hand side. There is parking opposite.

Refreshment: There are bars and restaurants in Porspoder and at Argenton.

Notes: This is a walk on good coastal paths for which trainers would be quite suitable in summer. There is little shade, so on hot days you should think of protection from the sun. Is it possible to bathe at Porspoder and the Anse de Penfoul – but note that the seas here are often more suitable for surfers than swimmers.

Waymarking: The coastal path is marked with the white on red flashes of the Grande Randonnée. Inland the path is waymarked in yellow.

Introduction

The north-west coast of Finistère is as dramatic, and the seas as turbulent, as one might expect from shores facing the mighty Atlantic. It is also incredibly beautiful. This is the country of the Abers, long tidal estuaries formed when sea levels rose at the end of the Ice Age. Unlike the estuaries of the north coast, these are not fed by major rivers but by tiny streams, and their sides slope less steeply while their beds are less deep. The abers face west, and are said to be at their most beautiful in the evening, when their waters reflect the rays of the setting sun. In day time, a thousand boats bob on the full tide, making another attractive scene. Between the abers, the coast is rocky and indented, with long bare promontories and off-shore reefs and islands. There are harbours shielding boats from the Atlantic gale, and surprisingly, occasional beaches of glorious white sand.

Perhaps in keeping with the landscape, this is an area rich in prehistory, and particularly in menhirs. There are so many of these that they seem to attract little local attention – the menhir you pass on this walk is all of 7 metres high, but it stands unmarked in a field where the

The chapel of St Gonvel

farmer has carefully ploughed and sown around it. Nearby are two other menhirs of even greater dimensions and many lesser ones are dotted around the countryside. With so many of these great stones to hand, there has been much scope for their investigation here. Are they in straight lines? And at what angle to each other? Are they clustered at high points, are they marking ancient cross-roads? There are no absolute answers, but if you are interested, this is the place to be.

This walk follows a short section of the coastline between the abers, north of the small town of Porspoder. Before you set off you can choose to walk up to the Pointe de Garchine, where from a high point with an orientation table, you have a view over the whole rugged coast and white-flecked ocean. From here the coastal path, the GR34, leads you on to the island of St Laurent and around the harbour at Argenton. Further on, you can divert to the little chapel of St Gonvel and the adjacent dolmen beneath a hawthorn tree before you walk on beside a long rocky bay. Contrasting with this are the white sands of the pretty Anse de Penfoul, a bay that attracts surfers at low tide. The return is over high ground, and from here you can again view the coast – and get a cross-field view of the lonely menhir of Kerhouézel.

The Walk

1. If you wish to start immediately on the route, take a track behind the church that leads down to the shore. If you would first like to see the view from the orientation table, it will add about half an hour to your journey. Keep the church on your right and turn left, following the signs to GR 34 and then the *Table d'Orientation*. Coming to the top of the hill, you turn right towards the coast. From the orientation table you can see near at hand the Presqu'il

St Laurent and behind it the Presqu'il du Vivier. Out to sea is the Ile d'Yoc'h. Now turn right and continue on the coastal path. At one point you reach a hard-surfaced road, which you follow for a short distance before leaving on the left again. The path passes a lavoir (an old washing place) and soon again comes close to the church at Porspoder (join here if you have not visited the orientation table). Following the white on red waymarks, you then swing left towards the 'peninsula'. St Laurent is in fact, virtually an island as it is connected merely by a narrow causeway. The path heads for this causeway and crosses it, after which you turn left to begin the tour of the island.

2. There are views of the Phare du Four (lighthouse) out to sea. You may be able to distinguish the ruins of a chapel, a cromlech and a menhir together near the far shore. Afterwards, the path passes an old blockhouse (look-out) and continues along the north shore to the causeway. Now bear left and take a track across the grassland behind the shore. Cross the road going out to the Presqu'il du Vivier and continue ahead, joining a road leading to the port at Argenton. Here you cross into a sandy alley and follow the waymarks, which lead you to the road alongside the harbour wall. As the road swings left to reach the Centre Nautique, take the road on the right the Rue des Amiraux. This leads to another track skirting a pretty bay and soon you reach a tarmacked road beside a little car park, where you turn left.

3. In about 200 metres, where the road turns sharp right, the *Sentier Côtier* leaves the road and continues ahead. If you want to see the dolmen and church of St Gonvel, continue on the road for about 250 metres to where first the dolmen and then the church are situated on the left-hand side. Retrace your steps to resume the coastal path, which now skirts a rocky bay and looks across to the Ile d'Yoc'h, the site of yet another prehistoric tomb. The *Sentier Côtier* briefly joins a road in St Gonvel, but then turns left again and looks out across the reefs to where a long digit of rock points out to sea. Beyond the outcrop is sand – the fine white sand of the Anse de Penfoul – but the sea will cover it if the tide is high. The path turns inland beside the attractive estuary. Just before reaching the road at its head, you are suddenly directed left across the top of the beach and then on a path under the trees to a car park.

4. Now leave the Grande Randonée going left to Kersaint, and instead keep ahead on the main road. After about 100 metres, take the small road on the right, now following yellow waymarks. At the T-junction, turn right. Coming to a farm on the left, do not go straight ahead, but bear left and, passing the house, turn right on a track alongside the hedge. Continue ahead on this track for perhaps 800 metres before reaching a tarmacked road. Now turn

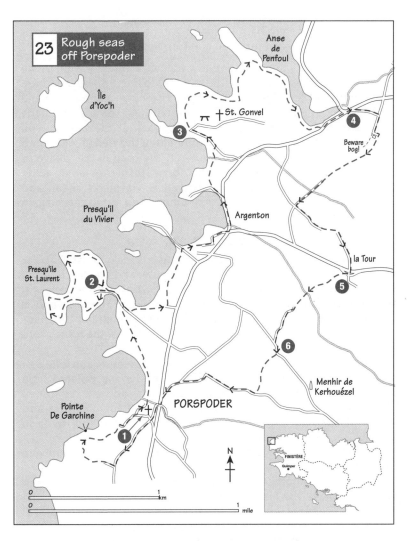

23 Rough seas off Porspoder

Anse de Penfoul

Île d'Yoc'h

St. Gonvel

3

4

Beware bog!

Presqu'il du Vivier

Argenton

la Tour

Presqu'île St. Laurent

2

5

6

Menhir de Kerhouézel

Pointe De Garchine

PORSPODER

1

N

FINISTÈRE

Quimper

0   1 km

0   1 mile

left, signposted to *la Tour* and the *Château d'Eau*. Where the track forks, do not continue ahead to the water tower, but bear right. This now brings you to the main road at la Tour.

5.   Cross straight over this road to the lay-by, and turn right off the road immediately behind it. There are no waymarks and the rather overgrown sunken path may look a little unlikely – but things will improve as you go. First though, you must cross a rather boggy area where a stream descends – the compensation is the beautiful display of wild flowers. After this you join a track coming in from the right and continue downhill on a much-improved track to cross the stream. Continuing ahead, the track reaches a

house and becomes hard-surfaced. After a further 300 metres or so, you reach a road junction and turn left.

6. In a further 100 metres, the yellow waymarks direct you off to the right. If you now wish to see the menhir, do not turn, but continue on the road for about 300 metres. The huge menhir is in the middle of a field on your left – but you will have to view it from the hedge. Returning to the waymarked track at the corner, you immediately bear left and continue along the hedge with good views over the coast. The track meets the road in the village of Kerdelvas, and here you turn right. About 100 metres along, at the sharp left-hand bend, ignore the yellow waymarks ahead and keep to the road. At the 4-way junction, keep left to reach again the church at Porspoder

More Walks in the Area

The GR 34 continues north and south along this rocky coast. Circular walks have been waymarked all along its route, and are described in the Topoguide *Le Pays d'Iroise à Pied (Ref. P295)*. This attractively laid out book contains some really excellent walks in the area and is well-worth seeking out. It is published only in French but the maps and waymarking are first-class, allowing you to follow the routes with no difficulty.

The next circuit to the north is about the same length, and follows a more open coastline with higher cliffs. It passes the isolated little chapel of St Samson overlooking the rough seas and visits the ruined 14th century Château de Trémazan, associated with much history and legend. It was said to be the landing place of Tristan and Isolde in Brittany – and as such has a heart-shaped hole in the wall. If you can manage a long walk, you could even combine this circuit with the one described in the text – a total distance of about 22km

To the south, another interesting circuit is that along the northern wooded shore of the beautiful Aber Ildut. The route starts from the mouth of the aber at the Rocher du Crapaud (Toad Rock) and passes Lanildut, a port whose prime export is seaweed.

If you are interested in menhirs, there are several circuits visiting some of the area's largest specimens. On the short circuit passing Kerloas (9.5m high), you also pass a high viewpoint with picnic benches and an orientation table.

Another Topoguide relating to this area is one which is also published in English. *The Path of the Lighthouses (Ref 059)* gives several circular walks as well as the route of the coastal Grande Randonnée 34 between Brest and Portsall. This long-distance route has views of no fewer than 23 lighthouses, of which the one on the Île Vierge is the tallest in France at 82.5m.

Places of interest nearby

If you have not time to walk along the coast north of the Anse de Penfoul, you should at least drive it. There is a fine outlook to sea all the way and you pass the lonely chapel of St Samson beside the road. It is always open and if you get out to explore, look also for the calvary and the *fontaine* or well, over to its left. Continuing, you come to Trémazan with its view over the Île Verte and the port at Portsall. The road passes the ruined castle associated with the Tristan and Isolde legend and haunted by St Haude (holding her head in her hands!). Her fate is a sad story, but if you can't meet the ghost in person, you can see her statue in similar posture in the chapel of Kersaint in Landunvez. Beyond Trémazan the road curves past Portsall, and on a headland with a view you can find the Dolmen of Guilligui. Dating from 600 BC, it is one of the oldest in Brittany. Travelling north to Porsguen, you can find in the harbour the anchor of the Amoco Cadiz, the oil tanker that left its horrific legacy to this coast in 1978. Just out to sea is the Île Carn, where there is a huge prehistoric cairn similar to the one at Barnenez. Farther on are the abers, Aber Benoit and Aber Wrac'h, both very beautiful. The lighthouse on the Île Vierge guards the rocky shores.

The menhirs in these parts are remarkable. Kerhouézel was passed on your route, but the biggest menhir of all is just a few kilometres south-east at Kergadiou. This one unfortunately has fallen down, but it is about 11 metres in length and weighs about 60 tons. Still standing close beside it is a lesser one, a mere 8.8m high. Again there are no signs, you will have to find them yourself. They are marked on the map of the region, close to the hamlet of Kergadiou. Farther south again, south of the D5 from St Renan to Plouarzel, is the menhir of Kerloas. Nicknamed *le Bossu* (the hump-back) it is 9.5 metres high, the highest standing menhir in France. This time there are a few (not very prominent) signposts to lead you to it. Its location, its alignment with other menhirs and the distances separating them have been the subject of much discussion and argument. It is certainly possible that the placing of these stones is not random but rather based on mathematical and astrological calculation.

24. Climbing Ménez-Mikel

In the lonely landscape of the Monts d'Arrée, the chapel on the summit of Ménez Mikel is a landmark visible for miles around. From here you can look out over wild moorland and the eerie peat-bog of Yeun-Elez – and then take a long walk home through the forest.

Grade: Moderate

Distance: 16km (10 miles) Taking the short cut will reduce this to about 12km (7½ miles)

Time: 5 hours for the whole route (which should give you enough time for a pause on the summit)

Map: IGN Série Bleue 0617 O

Start and finish: Car park at St Rivoal

How to get there: St Rivoal lies 5km west of the D785 Pleyben – Morlaix road, just north of the village of Brasparts. There is a large car park in the centre of the village, opposite the church.

Refreshment: There is a bar/restaurant in St Rivoal – but none en route.

Notes: Unless the weather has been particularly dry, this is a walk for walking boots. The tracks through the forest can become muddy, especially in winter. The climb up Ménez Mikel is quite gentle – as are later short climbs in the forest. All is on well-defined tracks. After about 10km you can choose a short return by road – but by continuing you will have some more fine views of the Monts d'Arrée, concluding with a pretty riverside path through the woods.

Waymarking: The route is waymarked in yellow throughout. The riverside path is marked with the white on red flashes of the Grande Randonnée.

Introduction

The Monts d'Arrée are the oldest hills in the world, formed in the primary era 600 million years ago, and perhaps originally ten times their height today. They are no longer 'mountains'. Wind and weather have worn the granite down to rounded summits (the Ménez), but within the granite is the harder quartz, and this has remained in places, projecting through in jagged 'teeth'. Such a quartz ridge is the Roc'h Trévézel, at 384m, the highest point in Brittany. Not far away is Ménez Mikel, a hill just 4m. lower but more conspicuous, its summit marked by a solitary chapel. All around is the wild moorland - wide empty spaces brightened by gorse and heather, barren heights, and valleys filled with woodland. Buzzards circle overhead and you may be lucky enough to glimpse deer – or even wild boar, although these are mostly nocturnal. This is possibly not at all what you expect of holiday Brittany. But the Monts d'Arrée have a beauty that is all their own

Ménez-Mikel

– and, being a part of the Armorique regional park, they also boast many waymarked trails.

The walk here starts from the grey granite village of St Rivoal. You could almost imagine yourself to be in Snowdonia! After wending your way through the forest you are soon climbing the gentle slopes of Ménez Mikel – or Mont St Michel, to give it its French name. The landscape seems so remote that, approaching the summit, you may feel slightly disconcerted at reaching civilisation in the form of a road. But the top is still a further burst of climbing away, and is unspoilt. And the view from the chapel is something you can afford to share!

Looking down from Ménez Mikel, the cloud shadows chase themselves across miles of bare moorland. To the east, often shrouded in its own mist, is the Reservoir de St Michel (also called the Lac de Brennilis), and around it, the desolate peat-bog of Yeun-Elez. Celtic legend has it that this is one of the entrances to hell. Exorcism was practised here in which an unwanted evil spirit was passed into a black dog, which was then drowned in the bog. This rather fearful spot has now, aptly enough, been chosen as the site of a nuclear power station. Turning your back on all this, a ring of summits lies before you – on this side the River Elez has its source, on the other, the River Elorn. If you have a really clear day, you should be able to see beyond the summits to the sea – the channel coast to the north and the Roads of Brest in the west. Down below, your path can be seen heading across the moorland to the forest – and you can opt for a short road return or a longer wander through the woodland with many heights and view-points, and an attractive stretch on the Grande Randonnée through the valley of the Rivoal.

The Walk

1. From the car park, take the D42 in the direction of Morlaix. Just past the bar/crêperie, turn right on the road to Bodenna. After walking uphill for about 200 metres, take the track on the left (waymarked in yellow), continuing uphill through the woods. Reaching the tarmacked road, do not actually step out on it, but rather turn back, and take the broad track to your right. This now descends again through a pleasant area of gorse and pines to reach a road once more.

2. At this road, turn left and walk through the little village of Bodenna. The tarmac now comes to an end, and you continue on a broad earthen track, which bears right and then left, but is well-waymarked. Soon the track climbs out of the woods and you have wider views. Gorse and heather line the path, with pine woods stretching into the distance. The route is obvious, climbing gently all the way – every track junction is waymarked, but essentially you are keeping straight ahead. After passing under the high tension cables and then keeping parallel to them for a short distance, you reach a multiple track junction.

3. A wooden signpost shows the first path on the left to be the *Circuit de St Rivoal,* while the second on the left goes to Ménez Mikel or Mont. St Michel. The latter is the one you should follow to the hilltop – but if you should want to avoid further climbing, the *Circuit de St Rivoal* will take you around the foot of the hill to join the route again on the far side. The path to the hilltop is broad, and after a few hundred metres bears left, picking up yellow waymarks again. Coming up below the road, you turn right up a narrower track to meet it. A signpost informs you that you are now on the *Circuit des Landes et Tourbières* (Moors and Peat-bogs). Cross straight over the road and continue climbing to the summit.

4. The chapel of St Michel was built here in the 17th century. Adding its height to that of the hill, the cross on its top is actually the highest point in Brittany. It can certainly be seen from some distance away – if you have taken Walk 20, you may have seen it from Huelgoat; if you have taken Walk 21, you may have picked it out from some 40km away, beside the Gorges of the Corong. The view from the chapel itself can be stunning on a fine day (don't forget to look for the sea!) – but unfortunately there are days when the mists arising from Yeun Elez obscure even the nearest view. At least it adds to the atmosphere of the place.

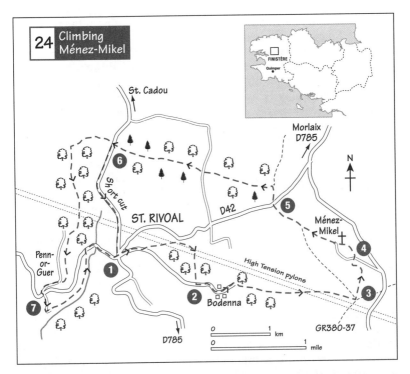

When you are ready to descend, continue downhill heading in the same direction – with your back to Yeun Elez. A flight of wooden steps leads you down to a car park. At the right-hand side of this there is a signpost – and misleading it is, too. It seems to offer only a circuit of the lake or a route around St Michel – but nevertheless, follow its direction! The track heads out across the moor vaguely in the direction of the radio transmitters on the horizon. The track skirting the foot of the hill now rejoins you from the left and you continue down to the main road, the D42

5. Turn right on this road, and after about 20 metres, sharp left, following the sign for the *Circuit de St Rivoal*. The path is again lined by pines and gorse, and soon you come to a corner with a field ahead where you turn abruptly left. Now the sunken track descends steeply to a stream at the bottom of a valley. Crossing a small road you keep straight ahead (there may be no waymarks here). The path soon becomes narrower and winds through pine woods beneath a hill rising on the right. Eventually (this section between roads will take almost half an hour) you reach a main road.

6. To return directly to St Rivoal, turn left here – you will be back in about half an hour. To continue, cross to the track opposite and

begin to climb again through the woods. Emerging at the top, you have fine open views of summits on the right. At the track junction, you go ahead and then to the left, again signposted as the *Circuit de St Rivoal*. The twists and turns of this route are all waymarked on granite blocks. At a T-junction just before the high-tension lines you bear left. The path is now quite obvious and well-waymarked as it descends through the woodland. After 25 minutes or so, you reach a small road where you bear left. This road soon reaches the hamlet of Pen-ar-Guer

7. At the main road, cross straight over to the waymarked road opposite. This descends abruptly, and, at a right-hand bend, you leave it to turn left on the GR 380-37. This is a very pleasant track through the woods alongside the River Rivoal. Near a bridge you join a hard-surfaced track and continue beside the river. Shortly the main road is reached, and here you turn right to return to St Rivoal. Look out for the traditional farm, the eco-museum *Maison Cornec*, on the corner as you come through the village.

More Walks in the Area

The Office du Tourisme in Sizun (or anywhere else in the Parc Naturel Regional d'Armorique) will, for just a few francs, sell you an excellent leaflet entitled *Circuits de Petite Randonnée autour du Yeun Elez*. The leaflet is essentially a map of this moorland area showing 10 waymarked circuits – the route of this walk was mostly on the *Circuit de St Rivoal*. On the back of the leaflet, each route is described in a couple of sentences – in French. But you will know from this walk that the waymarking and signposting are so good that you will have no difficulty whatsoever following these routes. A brave choice from this leaflet might be the *Circuit du Yeun* (16km), according to Celtic legend a tour around the gates of hell! In fact, it is a walk through a fascinating and fragile protected environment – just don't forget to stay on the marked paths. If you would prefer a little moorland with the peat-bog, the *Circuit des Landes et Tourbières*, which you briefly touched on this walk, is a very pleasant walk, and includes the summit of Ménez-Kador.

The Topoguide *Pays de Morlaix, Trégor et Monts d'Arrée (Ref 056)* covers this region and offers a choice of more than 40 walks. A less expensive production offering walks in the north of the region is *Promenades et Randonnées au Pays des Enclos et des Monts d'Arrée*. This is a series of 14 leaflets with two walks on each. The mapping is excellent – routes are clearly drawn on the appropriate sector of the IGN Série Bleue map – and the waymarking is similarly of good quality. If French is not a problem, the leaflets will give you lots of information as well. From nearby Sizun, a fine long circuit (19km) is described through the valley of the Elorn and around the Lac du Drennec. Various short cuts are possible and they are all clearly shown. Sizun itself has one of the most attractive of the parish closes (see below) and the Lac du Drennec has possibilities for swimming, fishing and boating.

Places of interest nearby

The Armorique Natural Regional Park has a particular wealth of eco-museums. This may be 'off the beaten track' country, but there is always something to do on a rainy day. Any Office du Tourisme can give you a brochure with all the details, but here are just a few nearby suggestions –

Since you are in St Rivoal, you should visit the *Maison Cornec* for a glimpse of 18th century rural life. The granite farmhouse has an earthen floor and an outside staircase to the hayloft. Living quarters were shared with the animals for heat, while outside in the yard stood the bread ovens. Stables and barns now display tools of the time and nearby is an old orchard of cider apples.

A few kilometres north, between Commana and Sizun, is one of the most interesting of the eco-museums, the *Moulins de Kerouat*. Here is a completely restored mill village on the River Stain, the buildings dating from the 17th century onwards. Houses are furnished in their original styles, from the poorest to the most sumptuous, in which lived a one-time Mayor of Commana. One mill is in working order, and amid much clamour and clatter, you can watch the machinery turning the millstones. Barns, outbuildings, stables, lavoir and much more are all there for you to wander around.

Another of these eco-*musées* is the *Domaine de Ménez Meur*, 6km away to the west. Here you have an exhibition centre relating to the activities of the Armorique Park, a large animal park with wolves and wild boar (at least you can see them here, if not on the walk), the Breton Horse Centre, nature trails, adventure playground and restaurant facilities – all adding up to a full day's entertainment.

At Brasparts, about 8km south-east, is an 18th century farmhouse which has now become a centre of Breton art and craft. Regional products are on sale and demonstrations are arranged during the summer months – although the centre itself is open all year.

Another outstanding feature of the Monts d'Arrée is the number of most elaborate parish closes – the combination of chapel, cemetery, calvary and ossuary all enclosed by a wall (see the entry under Walk 20, Huelgoat). It seems that the villages here tried to outdo one another with the capabilities of their stonemasons. Tourist Information Offices should all be able to give you literature about them – there is even a 'Parish Close Trail'.

25. Camaret and the alignments of Lagatjar

The old port of Camaret-sur-Mer is right at the tip of the beautiful Crozon peninsula. This walk climbs to the cliffs above the town, where lines of megaliths front the westerly wind and the tragic ruins of an old manor gaze out over a bay of golden sand.

Grade: Moderate

Distance: 12km (7½ miles)

Time: 3 hours

Map: IGN Top 25 0418 ET

Start and finish: Port of Camaret-sur-Mer

How to get there: The Crozon peninsula lies between the Bay of Douarnenez and the Roads of Brest. From Crozon, take the D8 west to Camaret. There is parking all along the sea-front facing the harbour.

Refreshment: Camaret is well-provided with eating places – including some pleasant sea-food restaurants along the sea-front.

Notes: Trainers would be quite adequate for this walk along well-defined coastal paths. There is no shade, so you should think of protection from the sun on a hot day – and take plenty of fluids with you. There are some fine beaches en route, but if you are thinking of swimming, remember there can be strong currents around this coast. Notices advise you of the risks.

Waymarking: The coastal path is a Grande Randonnée and is marked with white on red flashes. The short return path is not waymarked.

Introduction

Camaret-sur-Mer was for many centuries a port of some importance, hiding behind the Pointe de Toulinguet and tucked away from the prevailing winds. It is a port enclosed by a long 'jetty' on which stands a chapel – and, perhaps not surprisingly, a defensive tower built by Vauban. This spit of land – called the *Sillon* – is quite natural in origin, the tides and wind here causing a build up of rock and pebble that varied with the seasons. It is only recently that the *Sillon* has acquired its covering of cement and tarmac.

Camaret's importance was at its height in the days of the sail. The natural protection of its harbour meant that ships would take refuge here from the Atlantic blast or wait in these waters for the gale to abate before venturing into the Irish Sea. The taverns of the town acquired a reputation for being able to 'entertain' sailors during the boring delay! When sail became a thing of the past, the port became a centre of lobster fishing. Now the lobsters too have gone, the port has assumed an air of melancholia, with skeletons of old boats lying sadly on the shin-

The alignments of Lagatjar

gle. The largest of these is the sailing-ship *Antarctica*, once used by Jean-Louis Étienne for expeditions in the polar seas.

There is one other story that must be told about Camaret. It was the scene of the first attack by submarine – except that it never quite happened. In 1801, Robert Fulton, an American engineer living in France, had invented a submersible wooden craft propelled by oars. Leaking and difficult to navigate, it could stay underwater for only six hours – long enough to fix dynamite to the hull of a ship. The target for the trial was to be an unsuspecting English frigate moored in the bay. The submarine set out, but became confused in its direction. Meanwhile the frigate decided to weigh anchor and sail off into the sunset – quite unaware of its intended fate. The disillusioned inventor never tried out his submarine again, and it was to be more than seventy years before a successful model was perfected.

From the fascinating port of Camaret, the walk takes you first to a clifftop covered with wild flowers, where a Navy Signalling Station overlooks the turbulent seas. It also overlooks the wide sandy bay of Pen-Hat – but don't be deceived, this is no place for swimming. Behind the bay, the grassy cliffs slope up to the distinctive stark ruins of the Manoir de Coëcilian. At the turn of the century, Camaret had found favour with artists and writers. One of these was the poet Saint-Pol Roux, who built here a rather strange Greco-Roman style residence. It was destroyed in a terrible night of desecration and pillage by the Nazis in 1940. The manor also overlooks a vast array of megaliths known as the alignments of Lagatjar – Saint-Pol Roux of course wrote about them. 143 stones now are standing here, most of them in obvious lines – but it is known that originally there were many hundreds more.

Beyond the megaliths the walk continues past old blockhouses now imaginatively used as museums, and climbs to another rocky out-crop, the Pointe de Pen-Hir. Here a huge monument to the Free French Forces has a view over the sea from the Pointe du Raz and the Île de Sein in the south to the Pointe de Mathieu and the Île de Ouessant in the north. Below the Pointe itself, three huge rocks look as if they have been cast into the sea by a giant's hand. Strangely, they are known as the Tas de Pois – the Heap of Peas. The sheer cliffs are a favourite site for rockclimbers – and if you indulge in a little gentle rockclimbing yourself, you can reach the Chambre Verte, a grassy platform in the cliff with a fine view of the Tas de Pois. After all this excitement, it is just an easy walk along the cliffs and inland tracks to return to Camaret. And even if there are few lobsters in the sea now, you can usually find some in the restaurants beside the port.

The Walk

1. Follow the sea-front to the end of the *Sillon*. Continuing on the road, you will see a signpost to the Pointe de Toulinguet – and a warning that the complete Tour de Camaret will take you 6 hours 40 minutes. Don't worry, the walk described here will only take you half that time – but you can always decide to continue with the longer route if you have the energy! Following the white on red marks of the GR, pass through a picnic area and continue to climb. The path passes a little old fort pressed into the cliffside before reaching the Pointe du Grand Gouin with more excellent views. The path from here is well-waymarked – it descends to the road before turning off again to the right to climb to the Pointe de Toulinguet. Rocks, gorse, heather and wild flowers make this a very attractive headland. There are many paths across it, but whichever you choose, you should arrive at the gates of the fort – now a navy signalling station.

2. From the gates, walk across the moorland to the opposite side, where there are fine views of the sandy Anse de Pen-Hat and the ruins of the Manoir de Coëcilian can be seen on the hill behind. Follow a rather indistinct path along the edge, which becomes clearer as it descends across the grassland to the bay. On the final stretch you are kept between fences to protect the fragile vegeta-tion. Crossing the end of the road, you continue to skirt the bay. Now choose any of the tracks that climb the grassy slopes to reach the Manoir de Coëcilian at the top. Unfortunately, the ruins are much less attractive at close quarters. Take the rough road behind the manor to emerge on a tarmacked road. On the far side of this are the alignments of Lagatjar, their windswept grassland now sadly encroached upon by houses.

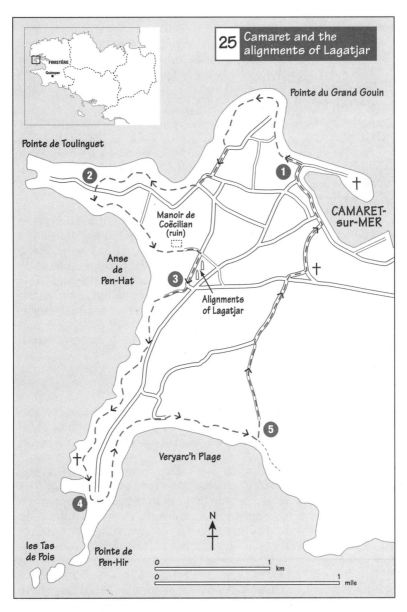

25 Camaret and the alignments of Lagatjar

Pointe du Grand Gouin

Pointe de Toulinguet

FINISTÈRE
Quimper

CAMARET-sur-MER

Manoir de Coëcilian (ruin)

Anse de Pen-Hat

Alignments of Lagatjar

Veryarc'h Plage

N

les Tas de Pois

Pointe de Pen-Hir

0   1 km
0   1 mile

3. Leaving the alignments at the far end of the field, cross the road again and find a track in the scrubland leading along the top of the cliff. Here you will pick up the GR waymarks again, and these lead you past the two blockhouse museums. The first is dedicated to the Battle of the Atlantic, the second to seabirds. The waymarks briefly bring you down to the road but then leave again to skirt the cliff on the way to the Point de Pen-Hir. Soon you come to the monument to the Free French Forces. A vast car park not far away accounts for the sudden influx of people. There is a fine view around the coastline. If you want to find the viewpoint over the Tas de Pois, look for a path to the left of the monument and viewing platform. This descends and then climbs to the left to reach a grassy ledge, the Chambre Verte.

4. Returning to the coastal path, continue across the car park to the far side, where a grassy track can be seen sweeping down to another bay, the Anse de Pen-Hir. Reaching the beach (Veryarc'h Plage), you pass a little café and continue along the coastal path again. After a further 15 minutes or so walking, the well-marked path crosses a hard-surfaced road.

5. Ahead the track is signposted to Kerloc'h – the continuation of the Tour de Camaret. But on this walk, you turn left and follow the track inland. Coming to the first road junction, keep ahead (slightly to the right) and at the second junction, keep ahead again on the Rue de Kermeur. This road now descends with good views over the harbour with the chapel and tower on the Sillon. At the junction with the main road, take the second road from the right, which leads to the church. Turn left in front of the church and keep straight ahead past the Mairie and the little square to return to the harbour.

More Walks in the Area

The whole Crozon peninsula is contained within the Armorique Natural Regional Park, and nowhere in Brittany is there so much fine cliff walking. The local tourist board have divided the coastal path, the GR 34, into five sections, each of which can easily be completed in a day. Each section ends at a place with overnight accommodation – but you could choose to use a taxi to return to your car each day instead. The bare bones of this 5-day plan are laid out in the leaflet *Presqu'il de Crozon – Circuits de Randonnées*, available from any Office du Tourisme. The helpful Tourist Offices at Crozon, Morgat or Camaret will also be able to assist you with accommodation or taxis – don't hesitate to ask!

The Topoguide *Le Ménez-Hom Atlantique à pied (Ref. 293)* offers you a selection of circular walks on the peninsula. This is one of the newer Topoguides, well laid out, with lots of interesting information (in French) – it can be found in most Tourist Offices and bookshops. But if you are looking for just the odd walk in the area, the Office du Tourisme in Camaret (or anywhere else in the Park) will sell you any individual route from this Topoguide, printed on thin card. The combined maps and waymarking make these routes easy to follow.

There is so much good walking here that it is very difficult to pick out any particular walks from this set. But you must visit Morgat (said to be the 'Pearl of the Crozon') and starting from here there is a route that gives you a bit of everything. The 16km circular walk is entitled *De la Baie de l'Océan* – and it does just that, crossing from the high cliffs facing the Baie de Douarnenez to the long sandy Plage de la Palue, looking to the Atlantic. In between is moorland, forest and river valley – a first-class tour of the southern part of the peninsula.

Places of interest nearby

The islands of Sein, Molène and Ouessant are visible from the Pointe de Pen-Hir – in fine weather.. If you would like to visit them, the company Finist'mer runs trips during high season. The Office du Tourisme should be able to give you details.

More boat trips start from Morgat where you can cruise around the rocky Cap de la Chèvre or cross the bay to Douarnenez. More popular are the boat trips to the nearby caves at each end of the beach. Scooped out of the multi-coloured rock, these caves are quite spectacular, with 'chimneys' to the clifftops high above. Morgat is also blessed with lesser caves, which can be reached on foot at low tide.

It is well worth heading out to the Cap de la Chèvre just for its superb views. The point is about 6km from Morgat by road – but a better option is to take the well-marked coastal path. The point is occupied by a Naval Station, but you can walk around this to a viewpoint with a telescope. From here you can see all around the Bay of Douarnenez with its beaches and headlands, from the Pointe de Pen-Hir behind you, to Cap Sizun, the Pointe du Raz and the Île de Sein. Walking around the cape, you can see that all the bay is under the watchful eye of Ménez-Hom, looming above the sands of Pentrez-Plage. The view from the summit of this 'mountain' is definitely one of the finest in Brittany – you can't miss Walk 28.

26. Around the Pointe du Raz

Wild seas and reefs off the Pointe du Raz made it a one-time favourite haunt of wreckers. Now this windswept westerly point is popular with the tourists – but take this walk around the high cliffs and you are likely be facing the elements alone.

Grade: Moderate (but you will need a head for heights!)

Distance: 8km (5 miles)

Time: 2½ hours

Map: IGN Top 25 0419 ET. But you can get an excellent free walking map entitled *Plogoff – Pointe du Raz* from the information centre at the point.

Start and finish: Car park at the Pointe du Raz

How to get there: From Audierne, take the D784 west to the Point. From Douarnenez, the D2 will take you there also.

Refreshment: The Visitor Centre at the Pointe du Raz sports an assortment of restaurants, crêperies, cafés and ice-cream stalls. You simply cannot be hungry here!

Notes: This walk is mostly on fairly narrow paths along cliffs high above the sea. It is not really suitable for young children. The paths are firm underfoot and trainers should be adequate footwear in good weather. The cliffs are exposed to wind and rain – it is best to choose a fairly calm day. And if the sun is shining, remember that there is no shade on the route. It would also be sensible to carry fluid in hot weather. And don't forget binoculars for the magnificent views.

Waymarking: The coastal path is the GR 34, waymarked in white on red, but the whole route is additionally marked with yellow flashes.

Introduction

The Pointe du Raz is to Brittany what Land's End is to Cornwall. This is the farthest point you can reach, a point where the setting sun sinks far out into the sea. Like Land's End, it attracts its visitors. A centre with shops and refreshments caters for the hordes – but tastefully it is sunken in a hollow and set back from the Point itself. Cars are not allowed past the centre, so to reach the point, visitors must take a walk of around 15 minutes, or catch the *navarre*, the shuttle bus. To be accurate, the Pointe du Raz is not quite Brittany's most westerly point (that distinction just belongs to the Pointe de Corsen near Brest), but it does have all the right attributes! The Pointe du Raz is at the very tip of the Cap Sizun, a long triangular finger of land reaching far into the Atlantic below the Bay of Douarnenez.

The Pointe itself is a high rocky outcrop capped by gorse and heather. Far below, wild foaming seas crash against the dark rocks and all around, the air is full of seagulls blown on the wind. On a clear day, the tiny Île de Sein can be seen squatting low on the horizon. Raz

Seascape near the Pointe du Raz

means Race, and it is well-named, for between here and Sein the tide hurries at a great pace and the currents are treacherous. This is a passage much feared by sailors. High on the Point stands the enormous statue of Notre Dame des Naufrages (Our Lady of the Shipwrecks) – an effigy of a half-drowned mariner reaching for the hands of the infant in Our Lady's arms. There is something rather tongue-in-cheek about all this, since until fairly recent times, the local population supplemented their livings quite considerably by pilfering from the wrecks.

The walk sets out from the Point along the southern side. Here you are immediately struck by the prevailing winds from the Atlantic. But the cliffs are bright with gorse and heather and soon you see far below you the tiny Port Bestrée, the high wall shielding a few brave boats from the Atlantic gale. Farther along you follow a wild coast of rocks and reefs before crossing the peninsula. Your first sight of the north side is surprising. Foaming white waves crash on to a wide bay of golden sand. A hotel in delicate pastel shades stands beside. All belies the sinister nature of this spot – this is the Baie des Trépassés, the Bay of the Dead! An explanation for this rather ominous appellation seems to be that with the predominant current, bodies of mariners drowned off the Île de Sein are naturally washed up in this bay. An alternative reason is possibly that, many centuries ago, the bodies of dead druids were ferried from here to their traditional burial place on the Île de Sein. Being Brittany, there are also stories of unidentified boats with lone sailors passing in the night and references to Ankou,

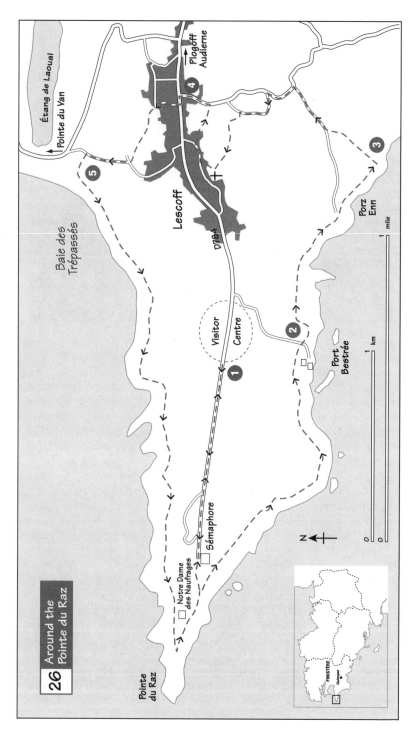

26 Around the Pointe du Raz

Pointe du Van

Étang de Laoual

Plogoff
Audierne

④

⑤

Lescoff

Baie des
Trépassés

D784

Porz
Enn

③

Visitor
Centre

①

②

Port
Bestrée

Sémaphore

Notre Dame
des Naufrages

Pointe
du Raz

N

1 mile

1 km

FINISTÈRE

Quimper

the grim reaper. On a sunny day here, you just can't believe it – but visit this spot in a winter storm!

In addition to all this, one of the most famous Breton legends of all time is associated with the lake behind the Baie de Trépassés, the Étang de Laoual. It is a legend with perhaps just a small grain of truth in it. In the 6th century, the Breton capital was the beautiful island city of Ys. The island was low-lying, and the city was protected from the sea by huge gates which were kept locked – King Gradlon himself kept the key. King Gradlon had a daughter, Dahut, and she fell in love with a handsome young man – who turned out to be the devil in disguise. The devil persuaded Dahut to bring him the key to the sea gates, which he then opened. The sea rushed in, Gradlon pulled Dahut on to his horse and fled before the torrent. A voice told him to drop his wicked daughter into the sea to ensure his escape and that of his people. Dahut thence became a mermaid, haunting the oceans and luring sailors to their doom, while Gradlon established his new capital in the town of Quimper. Ys remains covered by the waves. Bretons have no doubt about the existence of Ys – and there is actually some evidence. The only problem is where! The most popular supposition is in the Bay of Douarnenez, but other contended spots are here in the Baie des Trépassés, off the Pointe de Penmarc'h and in the Bay of Erquy.

As you descend the road to the bay, you can contemplate what lies beneath the waters of the lake. But when you turn to go home, you will need to keep your eyes firmly on the ground as the path gets trickier as you go. When you finally round a headland where the cliff ahead seems impossible, you are suddenly spared further difficulties as the path turns inland. In a few minutes, you are looking across the heather to the *sémaphore* and statue on the headland, a scene teeming with people once more.

The Walk

1. Leaving the car park, cross to the information bureau at the end of the line of shops. Behind it is the bus stop for the shuttle and the start of the path out to the Point itself. After about 10 minutes walking on the well-used path, you reach the signal station and the statue of Notre Dame des Naufrages. The rocky tip is still ahead of you – explore it now or at the end. To follow the walk, bear left (sea on right) on a wide track across the cliff top. After a few minutes walking the track forks. Take the narrow right-hand path, signed as the *Sentier Côtier*. This heads off along the side of the cliff with spectacular views all the way. The path is quite obvious until you reach a fork with a tarmacked road ahead. The right-hand path now goes down to Port Bestrée and it is well worth taking a look down there! The left-hand path continues to the road – the road to the port.

2. Whether or not you went down to the port, you will arrive at the point at which the coastal path crosses the road. From here, continue on the coastal path again, following the waymarks. There is a fine view ahead and the path soon passes an arch through the rock as it winds around to a little cove. At this cove, do not take the path ahead, but continue on the coastal path, which climbs again. The coastal path soon passes a pebbly cove, Pors Enn, and then ascends the cliff once more. At its height, the yellow waymarks direct you to leave the Grande Randonnée and turn inland.

3. Now following the track across the rough grassland, you reach a hard-surfaced road. Turn right and follow this to the village. At the road junction beside the first houses, turn left, uphill. Now take the first road on the left, which soon turns a sharp corner to the right. Ahead of you at this corner are two traditional low stone fishermen's cottages. After passing the calvary, take the first earth track on the left. This leads you downhill to an old lavoir on the stream at the bottom, and then climbs past the little stone Chapel of St Michel. Here the path bears right between walls to arrive at a square with another calvary. Ahead of you is a very old stone house with carving around the tiny windows and doors. Turn right, and after 20 metres, at the junction, right again, still following the clear waymarking. Soon you are on a track between stone walls, and at its end, you bear left twice to reach the main road.

4. Cross the road to take a road on the other side, about 50 metres to the left, just before the Lescoff sign. This road brings you to a grassy area where a track leads down between houses on the left. The track soon corners and levels out along the top of a field. At the next track junction, bear right, and coming to another lavoir, join the road to descend to the beautiful Baie des Trépassés – a curve of golden sand with the long Étang de Laoual behind it in the valley.

5. Before reaching the sandy bay, turn left, following the *Sentier Côtier* signs to a path running below the old blockhouses. This climbs with magnificent views of the bay as you go. The path is quite obvious – and at times quite precarious – as it clings to a cliffside bright with spring flowers. On rounding a headland and facing huge cliffs descending to the foaming sea, the path suddenly turns away. Very soon you are surprised to see the *sémaphore* and statue of Our Lady quite close at hand and you have no trouble following the path across the heather to reach the Point again.

More Walks in the Area

Tourist Information at the Point can offer you a little leaflet entitled *Plogoff – Pointe du Raz*. Three walks are shown on a clear map. One of these approximately corresponds to the walk described here. The other two are circuits of similar length, each based on a section of coastal path along the south of the peninsula. A French text accompanies the map, but it is quite easy to follow the routes without reference to this as the waymarking is so good.

The same map also shows the route of the GR 34 in the area – you could decide to follow it as far as the Anse du Loc'h (just beyond Plogoff, approx. 10km) and return by bus. The timetable can be found at the Pointe du Raz or at the Office du Tourisme in Audierne. If you feel you could handle something more ambitious, take the morning bus from Audierne to the Pointe du Raz and return on foot – a distance of about 24km along the most splendid shoreline. The Top 25 map mentioned above will show you the route, and the waymarking is excellent.

North of the Point du Raz, the coastal path skirts the Baie des Trépassés and heads past the remote Chapel of St They to the Pointe du Van. Although there is a big car park here, it is considerably quieter than its neighbour. From this point the views are quite magnificent – from the Pointe de St Mathieu near Brest, to the tip of the Crozon peninsula and across to the Île de Sein and Pointe du Raz. Beyond the Pointe du Van, the coastal path then passes a succession of headland viewpoints and among them, an ornithological paradise, the *Réserve du Cap Sizun*. No public transport serves this splendid north coast – you are on your own. But the Office du Tourisme in Douarnenez should be able to advise you about taxi services.

And finally, if you are staying for some time, you would do well to invest in this area's own Topoguide, *Finistère: Pointe du Raz / Cap Sizun (Ref. 291)*. Here you will find the whole route of the Grande Randonnée around the coast and a selection of short circular walks as well – a comprehensive walker's guide to the area.

Places of interest nearby

If you feel you can brave the passage to the Île de Sein, two boat companies make the one-hour crossing from Audierne. Decide which one you want to travel with – the tickets are not interchangeable. Sein is a low-lying treeless island, a mere 8.5 metres above sea level at its highest point. Twice in the 19th century it completely disappeared under the waves. The tiny island is now permanently inhabited by just a few fishing folk – although there is a village with two shops and a few restaurants for visitors. Once upon a time, the islanders made their living by plundering from the many wrecks on the low reefs around its shores. But wrongdoings of the past were forgotten in the last war, when every able-bodied man on the island set sail for Britain to join the Free French Forces. For this, and for the part it played in the escape of thousands more, the island was awarded the Liberation Cross.

There is not much to see on a day trip here – but it is certainly atmospheric.

The bird reserve at Goulien is open to visitors from mid-March to the end of August – the nesting season. Wandering along the paths on a cliffside scattered with wild flowers, you can observe cormorants, guillemots and a variety of gulls at their nesting sites. You will need binoculars – but these can even be hired at the reserve.

The most remarkable museum of this area is undoubtedly the twin Port Musée and Musée du Bateau at Douarnenez. In the old harbour at Port-Rhu, about 20 boats of all kinds are open for exploration – steam and sail craft, fishing boats and even a lightship are moored here. Back on dry land, a further 60 or more vessels are to be seen in the Musée du Bateau where they are worked on by traditional craftsmen. You can watch sail and rope makers at work, along with sculptors, painters and many others. A restaurant is provided for you to enjoy a full day out.

27. Wildfowl on the river at Loctudy

The wide calm tidal waters of the Pont l'Abbé River attract waders and wildfowl throughout the seasons. On this walk along the sheltered pine-fringed shores, you will also come across an old tide-mill and a partly-submerged menhir.

Grade: Easy

Distance: 11km (7 miles)

Time: 3 hours

Map: IGN Top 25 0519 OT

Start and finish: Place de la Mairie, Loctudy

How to get there: From Pont l'Abbé, follow the D2 south to Loctudy. Keep to the coast road, and the large car park is on your right, just before the port.

Refreshment: There are bars and restaurants in the village of Loctudy, but none en route

Notes: Trainers would be quite adequate for this easy route in dry weather. However, be warned that in winter, and after rain, the sunken roads taken on the way home can become rather muddy – choose your footwear accordingly. Take plenty of fluids with you, and on a hot day remember sun cream – although the route does offer some shade. And if you want to get a good look at the wildfowl, take binoculars.

Waymarking: The path beside the river is a Grande Randonnée and is marked with flashes of white on red. The rest of the route is waymarked in orange.

Introduction

The Rivière de Pont l'Abbé is at the heart of the Pays Bigouden – the south western corner of Brittany, named after the very tall hat of white lace, still worn by local women on festive occasions. This is a land steeped in tradition, its economy long based on the fishing industry. Loctudy, where the Pont l'Abbé River reaches the sea, is one of the main ports, and makes an exciting visit when the catch arrives in the early evening.

From the port at Loctudy you can look across the mouth of the Pont l'Abbé River to the little village of Île Tudy, just a few minutes ferry ride away on the far side. The journey by land will take a lot longer. Behind Loctudy, the river opens up into a wide flat expanse of tidal water with many creeks and inlets. This is a *ria*, a river valley flooded when sea levels rose many thousands of years ago – the river can still be seen flowing through the swamp at low tide. The vast mudflats continuously washed by briny waters and bordered by typical salt-loving vegetation are a paradise for the birds – herons, egrets, spoonbills, avocets, plovers, curlews, redshanks, shelducks and many others can

Menhir mouillé – a 'wet' menhir at high tide

be seen on the marsh. Winter is perhaps the best time for viewing them, when the river is also renowned for its large flocks of pintails.

If you have the opportunity, walk the length of the western shore of this river from Pont l'Abbé to Loctudy. In high season, a boat leaves Loctudy in the late afternoon and will return you to Pont l'Abbé in style. But since this is only possible in the summer months, and even then, not every day, the walk described here is a circular one and includes the very prettiest stretch where pines and deciduous woodland reach to the river bank. The views change with the tide – the wide expanse of water at high tide reduces to only that of the original river bed at low. The shores become green and brown with coloured algae and a whole new plant life is revealed at the edge of the mud. At one point you reach a tide-mill, and a little further along, a *menhir mouillé* – a standing stone out in the water. Six thousand years ago, the river bank was much lower than today, about at the level of present low tide. Now the great menhir stands half-submerged at high water, and fully exposed only at low. A long crumbling jetty gives you a last look at the swollen river before you leave to return inland. On the way you can pause to visit the eco-museum, a restored old farm at Kervaségan, before taking to the shady sunken lanes that will return you to Loctudy.

The Walk

1. From the car park, cross the main road towards the sea, and turn left. You will soon see the first white on red waymarks of the Grande Randonnée, which you will follow along the length of the river. At the roundabout, turn right following a sign to *Circuit de Laë ar Barez*. The road leads down behind some big houses fronting on to the water and then comes down to the dam across an

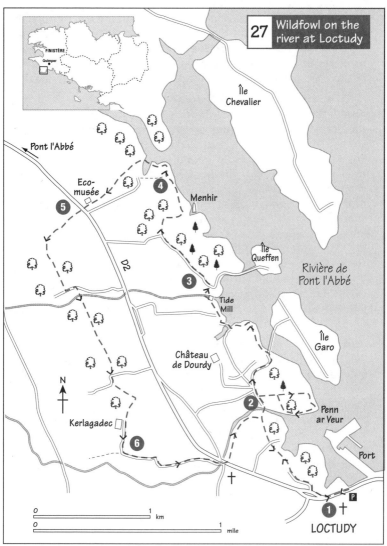

entrant river. Out to sea you can see the pleasure boats at the harbour. The track climbs on the far side of the dam.

2. Soon a junction is reached where you have the option of turning right to take a tour of the headland of Penn ar Veur with its fine views of the river. The path is waymarked in white on red and will return you to this same point to continue along the road, and then bear right in front of the entrance to the Château de Dourdy. The road now skirts a holiday village and arrives at the coast at the bridge to the Île Garo. The island itself is private, but you are permitted to venture on to the bridge. Turn left here, following signs to Queffen. The path now follows the edge of the bay through the attractive grounds of the Château de Dourdy. Ahead you can see the pine-clad little island of Queffen, a bird sanctuary. Shortly you arrive at another dam, this time with a tide-mill. Keep ahead beside the river and then bear right, shortly to reach a tarmacked road

3. Turn left on the road, still following the waymarks of the Grande Randonnée. Where the road takes a sharp left-hand corner, keep straight ahead into the woods. A signpost indicates that this is the *Site Naturel Protégé de Rosquerno*. A little farther along, at the track junction, do not continue ahead (S.P. Rosquerno), but turn right following orange marks towards the coast. At a clearing, the path takes a sharp turn to the left, but to see the menhir you should bear right here. A signpost directs you to the *Observatoire*. Emerging through the oaks and pines you have a lovely view over the calm waters to the Île Chevalier on the far side. Just off-shore stands the menhir, bands of colour around its thick body marking the extremes of tide. Turning away from the tranquil scene, return to the clearing and turn right following the waymarks of the Grande Randonnée. The path continues through the woods beside the river with views over the old jetty ahead.

4. Coming to a T-junction of tracks, the orange route goes left, but you turn right, still following the Grande Randonnée. This brings you down to the riverside at the end of the jetty – a fine viewpoint over the river. From here you turn left along the river and continue over the dam. Immediately on the far side of this, take the first track on the left and then bear right. This winds uphill through the woods where the occasional tree bears an orange waymark. After a bend to the left, you reach a T-junction where you turn right, again uphill. Now continuing ahead, the track runs beside fields and finally emerges in the car park of the *Ecomusée de Bigouden*, the Ferme de Kervaségan. Walk through the car park to the main road.

5. Cross the road and take a wide track opposite, a few metres to the right. This leads straight into the woods again, and soon bears left and becomes a sunken track between banks. It is waymarked in orange. The track continues ahead for over a kilometre, broken only by a bend to the left and then to the right near the Manoir de Pen ar Prat. Eventually a tarmacked road is attained, but very soon this bears right, and once again you plunge into the woods on a rough track. After 600 metres or so you reach the splendid flower-bedecked old farm of Kerlagadec, and with it, more hard-surfaced road.

6. This road soon takes a sharp left-hand bend, and here you will see orange waymarks on a track on the right. Ignore them. Keep on the road for a further 800 metres or so, to where it joins the main road at a roundabout. On the right is the Chapelle de Croaziou. Cross over to this chapel, and then cross the D2 directly to a broad track opposite, flanked by pine trees. The avenue leads to the Manor of Briemen, one of the riverside houses you passed earlier, hidden from prying eyes behind a high wall. When you reach it, turn right and retrace your steps to return to the car park at Loctudy.

More Walks in the Area

This fascinating area has a Topoguide almost entirely to itself – *Le Pays Bigouden et le Pays de Douarnenez à Pied (Ref 294)* – describing around 30 circular walks in the area. It is published only in French, but the maps are clear and the waymarking is good. This is one of the newer Topoguides and if you can lay claim to just-a-little-French-and-a-dictionary, there is lots of well-presented information to enjoy with the walks.

If you are keen to walk all around the Rivière de Pont l'Abbé, completing the circuit with the short ferry crossing, the 21km route is described in this Topoguide. It makes an excellent full day's outing. Other walks to appreciate are the circuit of the rocky Pointe de Penmarc'h and the walk along the seafront at the busy port of Guilvinec.. Inland there are walks taking in chapels, megaliths, fountains and lakes. Two short walks (5 – 6km) to be recommended are one including the Botanical Gardens at Raphalen and another in the south near Guilvinec where there are dolmens, an old chapel and three fountains, all within a few kilometres.

Topoguides are unfortunately relatively expensive (but much cheaper to buy in France than England). If you are looking for just an inexpensive booklet with a few walks in the area, the Office du Tourisme at Pont l'Abbé publishes *Les Circuits Découvertes de Pont l'Abbé et ses Environs*. The maps are sadly not too great and there is no reference to waymarking, but there is lots of informative French text. The most interesting circuit is perhaps that of the *Étang du Moulin Neuf*. Bird watchers will love it and the text describes every species you can hope to see – but don't forget your dictionary, as well as your binoculars. A more user-friendly cheap publication is the *Guide de Randonnées et du Patrimoine en Pointe Bigouden* – a big name for a little leaflet! This is simply an excellent map of the area around Penmarc'h, showing all the paths and places of interest. It can be obtained from the Office du Tourisme in Penmarc'h.

Bigouden has a varied coastline – to the west are wide sands and dunes, the point of Penmarc'h (literally 'Horse's Head') is rocky, while the southern shores are prettier with creeks and fishing ports. The GR 34 follows it all the way, and if you enjoy linear walks there are lots of possibilities. From Pont l'Abbé, you could take the bus to Penmarc'h and then take the coastal path through le Guilvinec to Loctudy – a distance of about 25km (16 miles). From there, return to Pont l'Abbé by boat – or continue on the GR alongside the river. The route of the Grand Randonnée is clearly marked in red on the Top 25 map named above – and, of course, the waymarking is excellent.

Places of interest nearby

Pays Biguoden is a land of seafarers and there is plenty of opportunity for you to take to the water yourself. From Loctudy you can cruise to Bénodet and up the picturesque Odet River to Quimper. You can also take a trip out to the Glénan Islands, about 10 miles out to sea, and spend a few hours on the largest island, St Nicholas. Even this will only take you about half an hour to walk around, but the islands again are a bird-watchers' paradise. The trip from Loctudy to Pont l'Abbé (the return described in the text) is provided by the company Vedettes Bigoudènes. As it is part of a circular cruise, it is unfortunately impossible to make the trip the other way round, or at any other time. The boat leaves Loctudy for Pont l'Abbé around 5 p.m. – but check with the Office du Tourisme at Pont l'Abbé before you set out.

Just north of Loctudy, on the road to Pont l'Abbé, is the Manoir de Kerazan. The rooms of this rambling stone manor have been restored to give an idea of life in its heyday in the 19th century. There is a fine collection of Quimper pottery – including a priceless violin – and pleasant grounds for a stroll.

A little farther up the same road (D2) is the eco-museum, the Maison du Pays Bigouden, that you passed on your walk. This is simply an old farmhouse, with all the associated outbuildings, tools and utensils such as you might have found here around a century ago.

Moving along the coast a little, the port of le Guilvinec is keen to show you its fishing industry in a discovery centre entitled *Haliotika*. High technology gives you an insight into a life of battling with winds and waves on the high seas – try embarking on a virtual trawler!

At the south-west tip of Bigouden is Penmarc'h. Not an attractive place itself, it is curiously dominated by the huge bulk of the Eckmuhl lighthouse – all 65 metres of it rising from a street near the sea front. The views from the top are magnificent – from the Île de Sein to Concarneau and out to the Glénan Islands. Closer at hand (just north) is the rocky Pointe de la Torche, and beside it some beautiful – if treacherous – beaches where windsurfers of amazing agility can be seen cavorting elegantly above the towering waves.

28. Ménez-Hom – a hill with a view!

Ménez-Hom looks out over the Bay of Douarnenez and all the ragged west coast of Brittany – and from its summit, 50 church spires can be seen. You could drive up here – but don't do it! There is so much more to be seen from the footpath. And when you have taken in the view, this walk takes you into a pretty valley where the sacred fountain has special healing powers.

Grade: Moderate

Distance: 13km (8 miles)

Time: 4 hours

Map: IGN top 25 0518 OT

Start and finish: Sainte-Marie du Ménez-Hom

How to get there: The village of Sainte-Marie du Ménez-Hom is at the junction of the D887 (Pleyben-Crozon road) and the D63 from the direction of Douarnenez. There is a parking area beside the road, opposite the church.

Refreshment: None at all en route. Take your own picnic – there is a picnic table in the pleasant grassy area beside the *fontaine* of the Chapelle Neuve.

Notes: It is a gentle but sustained climb to the summit of Ménez-Hom. The track is a little rough and you would probably feel more comfortable in walking boots out of season or in wet weather. Carry water with you as there is none en route. Don't forget your binoculars for the view from the top – and you might need an abacus for counting all those spires.

Wamarking: The route is waymarked in yellow throughout.

Introduction

Ménez-Hom is the last westerly outpost of the Montagnes Noires, almost an afterthought in the long ridge of granite hills. A mere 330 metres in height, its lack of altitude is more than compensated for by its superb location. To the west, it looks out over a scene where the bright blue Bay of Douarnenez is encircled by the green arms of Cap Sizun and the Crozon peninsula. Farther north, the roadstead of Brest leads out to the Pointe de St Mathieu, and to the south, the Pointe de Raz sweeps away to Penmarc'h. Turning around, there is a view of the estuary of the Aulne with the suspension bridge at Térénez and far away behind you are the Montagnes Noires and the Monts d'Arrée. On a clear day, the tiny chapel of St Michel can be seen over 15 miles away, on top of Ménez-Mikel, the highest point in Brittany. Bretons are always counting their church spires, but even so, the 50 or more visible from this spot would seem to be a record.

Of course, a place like this has its legend attached. On the north-west flank of the hill is a cairn said to be the burial place of King

Marc'h, the wronged lover in the Tristan and Isolde saga. After their deaths, King Marc'h became a tyrannical ruler – although he did establish the church at St Marie on the slopes below Ménez-Hom. It is said that his soul will be released to go to heaven when the cairn becomes high enough to afford a view of that church from its summit. Walking up this hill you may even meet the fair lady who invites wanderers to add a stone to the pile.

When at last you come down from Ménez-Hom, this walk takes you through a green valley where the *fontaine* has very special powers. Many of the remote churches in Brittany have a nearby *fontaine*, or spring. At each the waters seem to have specific powers of healing attributed to them. In this valley, the *fontaine* of the Chapelle Neuve is the place to bring an infant who is late in walking. First the child should be bathed in the waters (this is hardly all-year-round treatment!) and then sat on the little stone seat beside the well. Mother should then sit at the base of the nearby cross and call the infant – whereupon, he will get up and toddle over to her! The well, seat and cross are all in a pretty wooded site in the valley – and there is a picnic table not far away where you could take a break.

The way home is up hill and down dale, through ancient farming hamlets and past a dolmen with a view over the bay. And when you return to Ste. Marie du Ménez-Hom, don't forget to look at the chapel itself – a 16th century version of the one founded by King Marc'h. It is notable for its ornate calvary and triumphal arch – and for its balustraded bell tower, which took over a century to complete.

The church of Ste. Marie du Ménez-Hom

The Walk

1. From the car park opposite the church, cross the main road and take the D47 in the direction of Trégarvan. At the fork in about 1km, take the road on the left in the direction of Kergaoc. A further 200 metres along this road, turn left on a waymarked track leading into the woods. This track is well marked with yellow flashes and leads steadily uphill through the pines. Look out for a sharp left-hand turn uphill at one point – but again the path is waymarked on a tree just past the junction. The pines thin as you go, and soon you climb to gorse-clad moorland above them. At length a Grande Randonnée joins you from the right and you turn left to follow its white on red waymarks to the summit. The views open up as you go and you can see to the right the estuary of the Aulne with its suspension bridge. Soon you reach the *borne* – the concrete marker – on the summit. This peak is known in Breton as 'le Yed' and it is from here that the views are at their best, rather than the at orientation table a little farther on.

2. Just past the orientation table, walk down the steps and turn right, following the yellow waymarks and those of the Grande Randonnée. This is a splendid descent among the gorse with fine views over the coast. There are often a few para-gliders on these slopes to provide added entertainment. At the track-crossing half-way down the slope, take the track opposite, and then continue to reach a track T-junction near the road. Turn left to reach the road and cross directly over to a yellow waymarked broad track opposite. On reaching the pretty village of Coatérel, take the first road on the left, and at the next junction, where the GR turns right, continue straight ahead. This wide track bears left then right to climb again, and about 500 metres from the village, a wooden signpost directs you to plunge into the valley on the right to find the *Fontaine de la Chapelle Neuve*. You probably won't have a crawling infant with you, but the site is very picturesque and well worth a visit.

3. Retrace your footsteps out of the valley to return to the main track. Now continue uphill following the yellow waymarks to reach a tarmacked road leading to a farm. Turn left here and continue to another tarmacked road, which you cross directly to a pleasant track lined by pines. 300 metres or so along this, you reach a little clearing with a rustic seat and picnic table. Continuing, there are fine views over the bay on the right before you reach another road.

4. Turn left on this road (ignore the yellow waymark on the track ahead). You can see traffic on the main road at the top of the hill, but about 200 metres before reaching it, double back on a road on

the right. As you walk downhill again, you can see a dolmen in the field on the right. When you reach two pine trees beside the road, take the narrow track along the edge of the field to reach the Dolmen du Ménez-Lié. From here the intended route passes through the hedge just beyond the dolmen and then follows along another hedge to reach the road again. But this gets overgrown and it may be simpler to return the way you came. However you reached the road, now continue along it and as it corners right, look out for a broad track on the left. Taking this, you dip downhill into the woods and then bear left to climb again.

5. At the cross-tracks, turn right on a broad track. At first through gorse and then through pines and chestnuts the path descends to the hamlet of Ménez-Yan. At the fork at the end of the houses, keep straight ahead, and about 200 metres farther on, as the road bends right, take a broad grassy track on the left. After a sharp right-hand corner, this track descends to the farm at Penfrout.

6. At the bottom of the hill, do not go into the farm, but turn left on the road. Just past a stone house, the road turns sharply right. You take a track on the left here and again climb into the woods. This track soon corners right and continues to a cross-roads where you take the narrow road opposite. The road now climbs quite steeply for about a kilometre – the compensation is the increasingly fine view on the right, a view enjoyed by several desirable properties. When you finally reach the road at the top, St Marie de Ménez-Hom lies to the left and it will take you only another five minutes to reach the car park opposite the church.

More Walks in the Area

If you are keen to visit more chapels with their healing springs, there are several nearby circuits that will interest you. Starting from Lestrévet on the coast south-west of Ménez-Hom, there is a 10km route entitled the *Circuit des Chapelles*. This passes the famous chapels of Saint Suliau and Saint Côme, each of which has a spring said to have medicinal properties. St Gildas, to the south-east of Ménez-Hom, has a chapel and fountain and is the starting point for another circuit of 9km. Further east, near Châteaulin, is the *Fontaine de Saint-Laurent*, passed on an interesting circuit which also includes a long stretch along the banks of the Aulne with two locks. And further down the same river, yet another circuit starts from the *Fontaine de Saint-Exuper*. All these walks are contained in the Topoguide *Le Ménez-Hom Atlantique à pied* (Ref. P293), which you can find in bookshops and even supermarkets – and, as this is in the Armorique Natural Regional Park, the Offices du Tourisme of the area should all be able to sell you individual copies of the walks.

Another route worth a mention is that starting from Trégarvan on

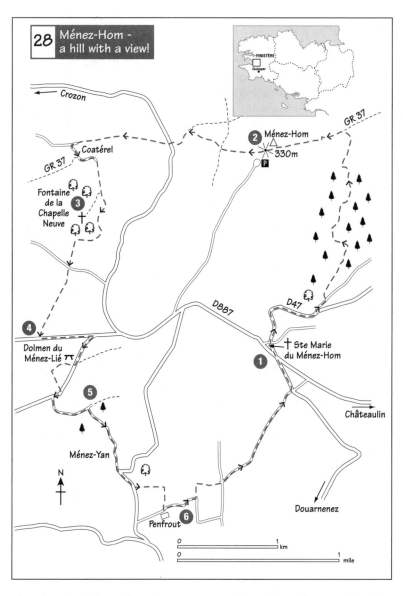

28 Ménez-Hom - a hill with a view!

FINISTÈRE
Quimper

Crozon

GR 37

Coatérel
GR 37

Ménez-Hom
330m
P

Fontaine
de la
Chapelle
Neuve

D887

D47

Dolmen du
Ménez-Lié

Ste Marie
du Ménez-Hom

Châteaulin

Ménez-Yan

N

Douarnenez

Penfrout

0   1
         km
0   1
         mile

the estuary of the Aulne. Trégarvan is a very pretty village and proba-
bly worth visiting in its own right, but the circuit of 12km also skirts the
Aulne and climbs to the moorland and forest on the slopes of
Ménez-Hom. The route can again be found in the Topoguide *Le
Ménez-Hom Atlantique à pied*.

The pretty town of Locronan with its well-preserved ancient
houses, is just 10km south of Ste. Marie de Ménez-Hom. Every six
years (next time in 2001), Locronan becomes the scene of an extrava-

gant Christian pilgrimage – a pilgrimage whose origins are druidic, but whose route of about 12km through the surrounding countryside follows in the steps of St Ronan, Locronan's founding saint from Ireland. This most elaborate and colourful procession is known as the Grande Troménie and attracts pilgrims and onlookers from far and wide. A Petite Troménie is held on each of the five interim years, the route this time ascending a nearby hill on another path taken by the barefooted St Ronan. These festivities take place on the second weekend in July and for the whole following week in the case of the grand Troménie. If you can't be here at that time, it is possible to walk at least part of the routes of the Troménies from a route published in the Topoguide, *Le Ménez-Hom Atlantique à pied.*

The Office du Tourisme in Locronan can find you an individual copy. This office also stocks a leaflet showing paths in the nearby Bois de Nevet, beautiful woods of beech, oak and chestnut. St Ronan himself lived in these woods in the 6th century, and it was from here that he set out on his walks, fasting and barefoot – every 6 days he took the 12km circuit, and on the days in between, a short 5km climb up the hill.

Places of interest nearby

About 10km east of Ste. Marie-de-Ménez-Hom is Châteaulin, a picturesque old town on a long loop of the River Aulne, which here is the start of the Nantes à Brest Canal. Here you can wander beside the quays and along the towpath and watch boats passing through the locks – if you want more energetic walking, the Office du Tourisme can again help you out with waymarked circuits.

Even when the Troménies are not in full swing, Locronan is a popular place – so popular that you are asked to leave cars outside and walk. Some 300 years ago, the merchants of Locronan made their wealth from the manufacture of hempen sailcloth. Now their old houses stand solidly around a cobbled square where the most impressive edifice is the 15th century church of St Ronan. There are lots of lovely old buildings here – but be warned, in summer at least, lots of people will be looking at them.

In the same series:

Each book costs £9.95 and contains a superb range of walks.

Available through all booksellers or direct from:
**SIGMA LEISURE, 1 SOUTH OAK LANE, WILMSLOW,
CHESHIRE SK9 6AR.**
Phone: 01625-531035 Fax: 01625-536800.
E-mail: info@sigmapress.co.uk
Web site: http//www.sigmapress.co.uk
MASTERCARD and VISA orders welcome.

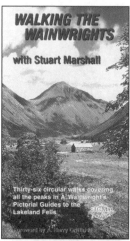

WALKING THE WAINWRIGHTS: A Field Guide
Stuart Marshall
This ground-breaking book is a scheme of walks linking all of the 214 peaks in the late Alfred Wainwright's seven-volume *Pictorial Guide to The Lakeland Fells*. After an introduction to the Lake District, the route descriptions are clearly presented with the two-colour sketch maps facing the descriptive text – so that the book can be carried flat in a standard map case. The walks average 12 miles in length but the more demanding ones are presented both as one-day and two-day excursions.   £7.95

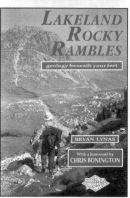

LAKELAND ROCKY RAMBLES: Geology beneath your feet
Bryan Lynas;
Foreword by Chris Bonington
This is the companion book to Snowdonia Rocky Rambles: the perfect way to learn about why things look the way they do. "Refreshing ... Ambitious ... Informative ... Inspiring" NEW SCIENTIST. £9.95

NORTH LAKELAND WALKS WITH CHILDREN
Mary Welsh;
Illustrations by Christine Isherwood
"It has been great fun speaking to children I have met on the walks and listening to what they have to say" says Mary Welsh. Her refreshing, enthusiastic attitude is reflected in her book, written specifically with the needs, entertainment and safety of children in mind. Perfect for parents of reluctant walkers. £6.95

See previous page for ordering information